ALTARS OF LIVING STONES

Building Faith One Testimony at a Time

ALTARS OF LIVING STONES
BOOK 1

PATRICK AQUILONE

The events and conversations in this book have been set down to the best of the author's ability, although some names and details have been changed to protect the privacy of individuals.

Copyright © 2024 by Love78

All rights reserved. No part of this book may be reproduced or used in any manner without written permission of the copyright owner except for the use of quotations in a book review. For more information, address: info@love78.org.

First paperback edition March 2024

Book design by Gerald, Adobe AI

ISBN (Print) 979-8-9902566-1-3

ISBN (Digital) 979-8-9902566-0-6

Unless otherwise noted, all Scripture quotations taken from the (NASB®) New American Standard Bible®, Copyright © 1995 by The Lockman Foundation. Used by permission. All rights reserved. lockman.org.

Permission to use obtained from https://www.lockman.org/permission-to-quote-copyright-trademark-information/

www.Love78.org

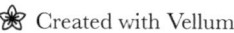 Created with Vellum

CONTENTS

DEDICATION

Standing on the shoulders of Giants.
- Mostly attributed to Bernard of Chartres

This book was conceived by and written for my children.

The intention was so they could know firsthand the full breadth of the testimonies Vicky and I've walked through, so they might build their faith and perhaps one day achieve more in Christ than we ever did and foster greater faith than we even could. We pray they will experience more of God than we ever did, standing on the shoulders of giants and casting bold visions farther than we ever dreamt was possible.
This is why I wrote this book, and to whom it's dedicated.

To Vicky, *my beloved and amazing wife. I can never express the deep love you have burned in my heart. You've driven me to be a better person by never accepting anything but my best. You have encouraged me to dream big, then reach for and fight for those dreams. Most importantly, you have shown me daily the great blessings God has brought into my life. I'm forever thankful to be called yours.*

To Katie, *our first: I can never express the pure joy you have brought into our* *lives. It was you who first made us parents. You showed me how love grows, expands and breaks out of barriers to enlarge and fill my heart. You've made me a better person by expecting the best out of me. You filled me with joy by just spending hours and hours enjoying my company. Katie, I'm so very blessed to be your father.*

To Abby, *our second: I can never express the pure energy and excitement you have brought into our lives. From the first moment you broke on the scene, you have been stretching me as parent in all the good ways. You have taught me how to grow far beyond my perceived capacity to love. You taught me how to be tender and loving by embracing my softer side, watching movies together (some that even made me cry). You have taught me to always be worthy of the trust you placed in me. Abby, I'm exceptionally privileged to be your father.*

To James, *our third: I can never express the pure love you have brought into our lives. I never knew I was missing a son until the day you arrived. You taught me to connect with my inner child, to relax and enjoy life. You showed me how to touch others for Jesus through your loving compassionate heart. You made me become a better man, just knowing you wanted to be like me. James, I'm incredibly honored to be your father.*

To Joshua and Isabella, *our children in heaven: I was blessed to get a glimpse of you and I cannot wait to hold you in my arms. It's my request of God that you will also receive a copy of this book to build up your faith and love and knowledge of the family that can't wait to one day meet you. To both of you, I'm grateful to be your father.*

HOW TO USE THIS BOOK

Before you begin, I want to drop a couple of quick notes about this book. Included are testimonies that are important to me, major events that have shaped my faith and formed living stones on my spirit's altar of faith, helping me grow in Christ. They may not have the same impact on you, and that's okay.

Firstly, this book was a pouring out of my heart and soul, with the intended audience being my children and grandchildren. God later told me to share these testimonies with everyone else for His glory and the building of everyone's faith. This simply means I wrote this from a perspective of sitting around an intimate campfire with my family. Since God has expanded the audience, I edited the book in a way to hopefully explain the events better, so anyone can read the words and understand the context.

Hopefully you won't be too confused, but if you are, I apologize in advance. Although I did write this with my family in mind, God guided my hand with you in mind as well. I don't know which parts will speak to you, but I do know God has a purpose for your reading this, and I'm excited for you to come on this journey and see where God takes you.

That said, here are a few **"dos"** and **"do nots"** with this book.

~

DO take whatever speaks to you and leave the rest. God uses different things to speak to different people. Some can hear a sermon and be inspired to become a missionary. Others can hear God while watching a movie and charge out to start a church. Still others can hear a song on the radio and be inspired to share Jesus at work. No one approach affects everyone the same way, nor does any one testimony impact people the same. Our God is a God of variety — not every testimony has to speak to you. Take the ones that do ignite your spirit and make them part of your spiritual growth. The ones that don't? Feel free to move past them. The goal is to provide a toolbox of testimonies that will be used by different people in different ways, building them up in the body of Christ in love. God only knows if a testimony you read today may be the thing you need to hold on to tomorrow.

DO NOT waste time struggling with belief. Neither God nor I would want your faith to be shaken by anything within this book. If you don't believe something you read, just move on past it. I love this quote from a professor at a Christian University, *"I'm not here to shake your foundations … unless your foundations can be shaken!"*

In other words, I'm not trying to preach to anyone or convert anyone or make anyone change churches or change your convictions. I'm just retelling what I've experienced personally, so that hopefully somewhere in this book is at least one testimony that will increase your own faith and help you when you're facing a trial. Don't let anything keep you from finding those testimonies, because one day your destiny in Christ will need you to have built up your faith. Seek God in the pages and you will find Him, then grab hold.

DO NOT waste time wondering why a miracle you've prayed for hasn't happened yet. I remember sitting a church twenty five years ago, listening to a guest speaker I'd heard several times before, recounting yet another amazing testimony and thinking "Man, I wish I had testimonies like that." And for years following that day, I kept asking God if something was wrong with me because I felt like I had no powerful testimonies or direct miracles I could tell other people about.

Looking back today, not only can I see how much God's hand has moved throughout my life, but I also have powerful testimonies, just like this man. The difference is back then I somehow thought he had walked out of his house and experienced no less than a dozen miracles a day before returning home, going to bed and then sharing them the following day as he did it all over again. Rise and repeat, day after day.

The truth is those testimonies were created over a lifetime of living for God. If you don't have any testimonies yet, that's okay. Just keep living for Jesus and doing what you know to be true (or anything God tells you to do) and one day you might just find yourself sitting and writing down a book like this, filled with the miracles *you* walked through.

DO pray before you read a testimony in this book. By doing so, you'll open your ears to hear from God. At the end of the day, it's much more important you hear a word from God than a word from Pat. This whole book points back to the Father, not to anything special I've said or done in this world. So pray that your ears will be open to hear Him, and then **DO** follow whatever God speaks to you.

My simple prayer over this book is that God speaks to you personally. One word from Him is worth more than the combination of all the gold, diamonds, gems and precious metals we could ever find on this planet.

INTRODUCTION

It was Thursday, June 20th, 2019, and I was having lunch with an elder from my church, discussing my walk with God and a dilemma I was facing over a recent vision. In the vision, I was standing on a shore with the most beautiful, inviting blue water in front of me. Jesus was calling to me to come in the water and join him, but I couldn't get in the water. No, that's not accurate. I *wouldn't* get into the water. I was too scared. Absolutely terrified.

So I just stood there at the water's edge, crying.

A moment later I was standing outside of my body looking at myself. I seemed to be a child of about eight or so just standing there as Jesus beckoned. I began to yell at myself.

> *"Why are you crying?"*   *"What are you waiting for?"*
> *"Just swim out to Jesus!"*   *"Please trust me. Swim out to Jesus!"*

None of this helped me as I stood there on the shore, crying.

I asked the elder if he knew what this meant. His well-meaning answer was "You have to step out into the water!" Now, this would be

13

great advice if it was clear *where* I was supposed to step out. "Where am I to take this step?" I asked. He had no answer.

I found it oddly strange to be given such an obvious, pat answer which honestly seemed pretty useless to me at the time. I was frustrated. Hurt. But mostly I was confused and scared, because I didn't like the vision of myself and I wasn't any closer to understanding it.

Before that point, I had spent many years not walking in the path God had for me. This isn't to say I wasn't in church or not walking a righteous path, just that the path I was walking was my own doing, my own design and creation. I had fashioned it out of what *I* wanted the path to be, not checking with God on if I was even remotely correct.

Looking back, I had foolishly not heeded the words of Abraham Lincoln, "*Sir, my concern is not whether God is on our [or my] side; my greatest concern is to be on God's side, for God is always right.*" The problem with my deciding how to achieve an end goal which God may or may not have set for me is I would inevitably find myself outside of the will of God, and therefore *outside of the protection of the Holy Spirit.*

God is far more concerned with my character than how fast I can scale a mountain in His name. This means the path from A to B is almost never a straight line. However, when *I* make the plan, it's the shortest distance between the two points. That's, until I fall headfirst into a pitfall or a trap or an ambush. It's easy to rationalize that others have taken the exact road, so therefore it must be the way. God would obviously want me to walk the exact path others have walked, right? Wrong!

I'm no longer able to count how many times I've been wrong second guessing the path that God wanted me to take. Each time I've chosen the path instead of walking on the path God would want me to, I found myself frustrated and confused and walking towards anything but my destiny.

I knew from a very early age that God wanted me to be a pastor and preacher. This meant that I would need to make my way through the leadership of a church on my way to my God destiny. I learned from several sources that the best path to becoming a pastor of a church was to start as a Children's worker because they always need help and there's always a need. From there, one could theoretically work their way up to the Children's pastor, and once there you might be able to hop over to Youth Pastor, and we all know Youth Pastors eventually become Associate Pastors, right? Then the Associate Pastor migrates to become the Senior Pastor of the church when the current pastor retires or becomes the Senior Pastor of a separate church plant.

Sounds super easy… in theory. Just get in at a low level and work your way up the corporate… um… I mean, *ministry* ladder, until one fine day — *BAM!* — *you* become the pastor.

Now, for some people this might be the exact path God used to bring them from Point A to Point Z. However, there was a problem with the way I was approaching it. What problem, you ask? God wasn't in it. I mean, I heard God tell me I was going to be a pastor. No question. But then I devised a plan on how to go about it.

The simple truth is if you want God involved in what you do, you have to let God design the plan. You have to let God promote you when He believes it's time, and to what position He wants you in next. Truthfully, you might never be a youth pastor. Or a children's pastor. Every person's road is different, and if we leave God out of it your goal will be empty and without power.

For me, I cannot tell you how many times I served on the Sunday School or Children's church teams where the position of Children's Pastor became open and I was unselected, unpromoted and confused. I was passed over, time and time and time again. And I, in my infinite wisdom and oh-so-spiritual maturity, wouldn't stop at simply crying before the Lord.

Oh, no, I would have words with the staff who didn't promote me, and when they inevitably failed to correct their obvious mistake? I would pick up my family and jump ship to another church who would better appreciate me and my gifts.

I was saved in a small church in upstate New York and, moves notwithstanding, thirty years later I've been a member of no less than a dozen churches. (Not to mention kicked out of one for assaulting the Associate Pastor.) A great track record of faith. A real resume of a mature disciple of Christ, and what a stellar witness to my children.

So there I was sitting in a restaurant, discussing with an elder in my church about all of this and more. I was dealing with a lot of things: offense (*how come I haven't been used of God or seen as important?*), bitterness/jealousy/envy (*how come that person God elevated in the body when I should have been?*) despair (*will I ever be used of God?*) and pride (*how come everyone outside of the church thinks I'm great and capable, while people in the church can't see the light of day?*).

I was a mess, and I felt like not only did everyone know I was a mess, but no one outside of my family really cared. This created a deep, deep ache inside me, a mix of earnest yearning for the things of God, combined with spiritual wounds which tossed me around like a ship battered by storm surges, fighting to tear me apart.

"…and that's when he began to talk about a memorial."

The elder finished speaking, breaking back into my train of thought like a train robber hijacking an engine.

"Who brought up a memorial?" I asked. "What does a memorial have to do with my issues? Were you even listening to me?" Granted, I had obviously not been listening to him, but his statement forced me to focus all my attention on him. I was somewhat in shock but listened as he continued.

"Pastor Myles brought up the Israelites and how God told them to take large stones and build a memorial," he continued, "so that when the children and grandchildren asked why they were there the elders could speak of all the amazing things of God."

While this was cool information, I was completely lost. Since I hadn't been paying attention, I had no context as to what this meant or why the elder was even talking about it. It was clear that he was sharing something about himself and his life that had culminated in the idea of a memorial. I had a deep feeling in my spirit that this was something important, something God wanted me to hear. However, it totally felt like I was trying to go to New York and the elder boarded the two of us on a flight to Los Angeles. Still, I continued to listen as he recounted a story from a recent family holiday dinner.

"I was sitting at the table and brought up a miracle that we [his wife and him] had walked through. I knew every one of my children at the table had been present when this event happened. I went around the table and asked them to tell me what *they* recalled about it, and I can't tell you how shocked I was at their answer.

"Each of my children had a *piece* of the whole story, but none had *the complete picture*. To make it worse, if we were to paste together the pieces they collected it wouldn't be enough to see the real power God displayed in that miraculous event."

He paused smiling. "We decided to share the full testimony with the rest of the family. Then we decided not to just stop there, but to continue to pass down our testimonies of miracles to our children and their children." He leaned in closer. "What we're now doing with our children is what the Israelites did when they planted memorial stones!"

When he said the words "Memorial Stones," for whatever reason I heard "Altar Stones." I didn't know exactly why I heard that, as I consciously knew what he'd said. However, in my mind the phrase continued to echo: "altar stones." I didn't say a thing, kind of brushing it off as me just being weird, and we continued our meal. While I nodded a lot during his sharing, at the time I didn't see anything in his story that pertained to me and my situation, specifically, and didn't give it the attention it deserved. Looking back, I regret this.

Today I try to look at every conversation with someone else as an opportunity to learn something, knowing the person I'm speaking with has information I don't have and I can grow from the exchange. At this lunch, I wasn't that man yet, and was mentally dismissing — albeit politely — any discussion that wasn't focused on me.

Eventually we finished lunch. As we were parting, he encouraged me that whatever edge I was on, I should take the leap and trust God, relying on previous testimonies to help me soar through whatever was ahead of me. I shook his hand, thanked him and went on my way.

When I returned to my car, as much I tried to push it out of my mind, I had two things swirling in my head. The first was whether or not my kids truly understood the testimonies we, as a family, had walked through. I was unsure, but resolved to talk with my wife about it. The second was the word "Altar" that would just not leave my mind, rolling around and around and around, nonstop. Just when I thought I had gotten on to something else, it would come back.

It got to the point it was so deafening, I genuinely couldn't think about anything else. I resolved to pray about it, albeit I was going to be more praying for God to remove the phrase from my mind than asking what He might be trying to say to me. At that point in my personal prayers, I was much more focused on providing God a list of demands or requests than I was taking the time to listen and seek out what He might be saying to me. This was all about to change.

When I got home, I spoke with Vicky about how the elder's children had completely missed God acting when it was right in front of their collective faces. We both concluded that our children were much more observant about these things, and surely wouldn't have missed God in the moments. She nodded a lot, and we finally decided we should put our theory to the test and talk to our kids about one of the largest testimonies we walked through: when God gave me new kidneys (*covered in full in a later chapter*).

Much to my dismay, our children faired about as well as the elder's kids. I had incorrectly assumed the elder's family missed it because they weren't attentive or maybe naive. However, hearing my own children having missed massive parts of our testimony gave me a new perspective. I quickly realized, in our misguided attempt to shield our kids from the reality that their father might die, we essentially kept them from seeing the full power of God at work.

Immediately I repented, asking for forgiveness. This was followed by Vicky and I sharing the *full* testimony with them that night, and they were all amazed at the power of God and thankful to Him for saving their Dad. We decided from that point forward to make sure our children (and *their* children) knew just how awesome and faithful our God was.

Saturday June 22nd, 2019

As hard as I tried, I couldn't get the word *altar* out of my head. It seemed to be around every corner, embedded in every sign, hidden in every lyric and popping up on every television show. It was literally *everywhere*, so much that it soon became super, *super* annoying.

After everyone went to bed that night, I cried out to God asking

Him to show me what this was all about. He responded to such a degree that I felt like He'd turned on a virtual firehose and drenched me with it. There was a lot to take in, but the biggest thing He revealed was the idea of an altar of living stones.

He showed me how within everyone's spirit's an individual altar made up of living stones, representing all the different events that have impacted and built our unique faith foundation. Living stones could be constituted of virtually anything. A timely word received from someone at just the right time. A miracle, either witnessed or taken part in. A scripture, reaching through time and space to make an immediate impact. How someone directly shared Jesus, either through words or in action. There's virtually no limit to what a living stone could look like! Yet each one represents a stone placed on the altar of our spirits.

God then showed me when He instructed us to build ourselves up on our holy faith (Jude 1:20), we essentially approach this altar in our spirits and recall all the amazing things God has done. This allows us to get our focus on Him and be built up in faith to handle whatever was coming next. God showed me the altar of living stones in my own spirit, instructing me to write a book with the largest ones to pass down first and foremost to my children, then to others to help build their faith as well.

The book you hold in your hands is the culmination of this journey.

Needless to say, I was blown away. Not only for the amount of information being poured into me, but for the fact He was providing me the very next step along the path. Immediately I knew what the vision of myself crying on the shore was about.

I had always wanted to be a science fiction or fantasy author. I absolutely loved the idea of crafting stories and creating worlds. I was about as far as one could get from writing a non-fiction book, let alone one based on the faith events of my life. I'd never once conceived of writing anything remotely like this, and yet God was calling out to me, beckoning me to trust him and come out to him, just like Jesus did with his disciples out on the water.

For a moment, everything seemed to align in my mind as the new knowledge saturated my soul like never before. Suddenly, I *knew* what God wanted me to do. I *knew* the path He wanted me to walk. I *knew* where I was going, the direction I needed to go.

All I had to do was to trust God and step out in faith.

Seemed easy enough. (*Hint: it wasn't.*)

About a week later I was worshipping, still marinating on all God had given me. I hadn't started writing the book yet, hadn't even created a template or opened my book writing program. Simply put, I hadn't stepped out into the water. As I was worshipping, I was taken in a vision back to the beach where I stood on the shore. Jesus was still there in the water, waiting patiently for me.

This time, instead of just watching myself, I was there, in my body. I took a very small step forward, just enough so my toes became wet. As soon as I did, Jesus took a step closer to me. Seeing this, I took another small step toward Him, enough that my heels starting to get wet. Again Jesus followed suit, although his steps toward me were much larger. Emboldened, I then took several more steps into the water until it was up to my knees.

At this point Jesus ran over to me. I was crying at this point, and reached inside my chest to pull out a blackish, semi-transparent ball, approximately the size of a basketball. Weeping, I handed it to Jesus, who smiled and accepted it. Immediately I felt free. Light as a bird, ready to fly and to soar.

I ran deeper into the water and splashed around as Jesus smiled and laughed. The vision ended, and I realized in that moment I hadn't fully trusted Jesus to be my God. Yes, I accepted Him as my Savior, but I didn't *trust* him. This is why I had to work so hard to make my destiny happen because I didn't trust God would do it if I didn't. When I handed Jesus the ball, I was handing Him my doubts, my life. I was handing him my everything, trusting that He would know how to handle it.

Since that moment, I've had days of walking fully in His arms and days where I snatched the ball back. But now I know that as soon as I catch myself doing this, I can give the ball back. Jesus is always so welcoming and forgiving to take it back and love me.

Writing this book of testimonies is part of my trusting Jesus. I'm stepping out in faith that God will guide me to write the complete truth and not miss anything. I'm trusting Him that my kids and grand-kids will read this and build their faith through these words. I'm trusting God that wherever this goes — including if it seemingly goes nowhere — that it will end up *exactly* where and how God wants it to be. I've put everything in God's hands.

Finally, it's my prayer that whatever God wants to impart to you as you read this book becomes a living stone in your own altar. I pray you will have your faith built up, empower and encouraged for what-ever God has in store for you in the future. I pray you will trust God with your everything. I can't promise that road will be without storms, but I can promise He will always be walking by your side through it all.

INFERTILITY TO BABY

'Then God remembered Rachel,
and God gave heed to her and opened her womb. '
- Genesis 30:22

"You can't have children."

You may have heard it said that the world crushes in around you when you hear devastating news. It's as if the very fabric of reality becomes a virtual vice, squeezing harder and harder, sucking your very breath and life out of you. Until this moment sitting in our Obstetrician-Gynecologist's (OBGYN) office, I hadn't known it could be so soul-crushing, so impossibly life-draining.

We had gone to this doctor because my wife, Vicky, had been having some difficulties with her woman parts — including, but not limited to, cysts. We'd known something wasn't quite right, and hoped professional insight could help us overcome whatever we were struggling with and get my wife back to "normal." Nothing prepared us for the moment when the world stopped turning and everything suddenly desaturated into dark shades of grey.

Life felt like an old time photo of things long since passed. Stark and lifeless. I honestly felt like I couldn't go on. It was at this moment that I was hit with a thought so dreadful it almost sent me into cardiac arrest. *How would I ever console Vicky?*

All my life I knew two things with absolute certainty. First, I would spend my life with a wife at my side. I knew from a very early age that I would marry and spend every moment after that in deep love, walking out the rest of my existence staring into her eyes. It caused me great grief when I first began to date and found that not everyone was interested in the idea of marriage or monogamy. Still, I continued to search until that one amazing day I met Vicky.

I knew that I *knew* that she was the one. Even better? She felt the same way. Life with her has been so worth living. Even in the valleys or the dark times, I wouldn't trade it for anything. She is my soulmate whom God selected for me before the foundation of the world.

The second thing that I knew was that I would be a father. I liked to think that I would be an amazing father. You know, Time magazine's Father of the Year cover material. National recognition or not, I knew that I was meant to be not just a father, but a Dad. I was meant to help shape and mold little ones into amazing adults. Like most pre-parent hopefuls, I had a list of things that my parents did great which I was going to mimic.

Dinner together every night as a family. Being ever present with my kids interests in music or sports or gaming or whatever. I had quite a mental list. I also had a list of things that I *wasn't* going to do that my parents did. Things like intentionally embarrassing my kids. By accident, undoubtedly, but I would never set out with the intention of making them embarrassed. I suppose my kids could tell you if they feel I was a good father or not, now that they're adults, but I did know from an early age that I would be a Dad, and I would love it.

You can't have children.

Hearing these words was almost more than I could bare. The doctor would later explain that Vicky has poly-cystic ovarian disease (PCOD), which caused her body to constantly form cysts which prevented and aborted pregnancy. In addition, the cysts would often prevent the natural monthly cycle from operating correctly, making getting pregnant almost impossible. The doctor probably went into more detail at the time, but honestly I didn't fully understand what he was saying. I was in shock. All I really heard was his words, looping over and over again in my head that *we wouldn't have children.*

I felt helpless, useless, an utter failure.

"However," the doctor continued after what felt like an eternity, "I don't believe a young couple like yourselves should be without hope!"

Hope.

Exactly what I had lost in his first sentence.

A person can move mountains if they believe there's a chance that what they seek is under it, even if that chance is minimal. Hope is a powerful emotion in which God operates constantly. It was hope I needed right then, even though I had no idea what the doctor could ever do to help us. All I knew was that one word, *hope*, my heart went from zero to sixty and I was ready to do whatever it took to fix this.

Immediately the doctor put Vicky on a drug called Clomid. This was to help spur on her baby making parts to…well…make babies. More to the point, the doctor felt that if we could "aid" the monthly cycle, then we would have a better chance at actually having a baby.

Next we began to chart my wife's temperature in the morning because, well, to be honest, at that point I had no idea. But the doctor said to do it, so we did it. Finally — and this was my favorite part — we were instructed to "work" at making a baby. We literally had a doctor's note instructing us to work at baby making, every single day.

It almost seemed too good to be true. An actual doctor's note declaring that we should become as one as husband and wife. It was the greatest thing ever! Well, that is, until it wasn't. With all spontaneity removed, things became passionless and mechanical and honestly, not nearly as exciting or enjoyable as I thought it would be (much to my surprise).

Coupled with all of the above, we had periodic blood work, urine check-ups and a bunch of other things monitored while we worked hard at baby making. It was an arduous process, and pretty well sucked the life out of us as days turned into months and months turned into a year. Before we knew it, we reached a place we never thought we would arrive: we were ready to stop trying.

When we started the journey, we were playful and excited and joyful about the process. Hopeful. But after a year, we were tired.

25

Working hard to plant seeds that produced no fruit. It was draining every fiber of our lives and our marriage, and some days it felt like there was no end in sight.

We felt discouraged. Disappointed.

But mostly we were just exhausted — mentally, physically and emotionally.

God walked alongside us the entire time, providing us with some much-needed help and encouragement in the oddest ways. Another couple in our church was also trying to have a baby, only both of them were doctors who knew all too well what was going on with them and us. If that wasn't enough, they'd been trying unsuccessfully *for over a decade*, and yet were always chipper and happy and full of love and joy.

We didn't know how they did it, but any time we were down, they were there for us. Their inspiration and love poured into us during the really hard times, because they knew exactly what we were going through. They were constantly pouring fuel into our tanks and helping us hit the gas. What's exciting is how God blessed them since that time. Last time we spoke with them, they had **four children of their own**. So God is good, all the time — even when we can't see it.

After almost two years of trying and charting and taking pills and getting poked and prodded every which way, one week my wife's temperature rose in the middle of her cycle and stayed slightly elevated. Those who have done this knows what that means. At that point, I thought it meant my wife finally produced an egg and we had somehow stumbled across the right mix. Now we could work on getting the egg fertilized and a baby formed!

We were at the doctor's office so often I don't remember how many days later, but I remember the next moment clearly. We had given all the chart information to the nurse as they did the usual urine stuff and checked Vicky's vitals, and then waited in the exam room for the doctor. I was excited because this was the first sign that something was working and God was moving! We were that much closer to having a baby! When the doctor entered the room I could hardly contain myself, I was ready to burst.

"Well," he said, breaking the tension, "It's iffy!"

"Okay," I gulped. "What is our next step?" I knew this was a first step in whatever process we were taking. I just didn't know what was next. I was thinking (dreading?) more baby making, complete with another doctor's note. But perhaps with indications of things moving in the right direction, some renewed passion and joy would revitalize our together times. I kind of had a dozen thoughts running through my head, but was working hard to keep focus.

"We do a blood test," he said.

"A...blood test?" I snorted.

A warm sensation washed over my face. I was fuming. We had painstakingly charted Vicky's temperature and done all sorts of circus acrobatics to ensure conditions had been *just right* for my wife's cycle to get on track, and now I was being told we could have just done a blood test the whole time?

A simple blood test. I was hot.

"You mean all this time we could have known with a blood test?" I clenched my fist, trying hard to control myself, but it had been a *long* two years. "What have we been doing all this temperature taking for?!!"

He cocked his head and squinted at me. "What are you talking about?"

What was I talking about? How did he not know? This wasn't the time to play dumb. We have been working together on this for *years. How does he not know?* And why would I have to explain this to him? "You think she finally ovulated!"

"No," declared the doctor, a smile dancing across his face. "I think she might be pregnant!"

In cartoons when a character is shocked or surprised, his mouth drops to the ground. At this moment in time, my mouth most definitely dropped to the ground, which felt like it was a few stories below my feet. You could have pushed me over with a feather, I was so shocked at his words.

So many things raced through my head, yet I sat there, unable to move or say anything. I caught a glimpse of my wife, grinning at me. I almost couldn't believe it. *We might be pregnant. We might be with child. We might soon be parents.* I was so overjoyed. It must have shown on my face, as the doctor nodded, flashed me a most ginormous grin and walked out of the room.

Back in these days you had to order a blood test and usually go and give blood at a hospital. Today many doctor's offices can take the blood right there and, depending on the test even test it immediately. Back in 1993, however, we had to make an appointment.

The problem? It was Christmas Eve.

They told us they were going to rush the results and they would likely take a day. Christmas fell on a Saturday that year, meaning we weren't going to find out the results until the next business day— Monday, December 27th.

It was the most excruciating Christmas ever! We wanted to tell *everyone*, but knew there was a good chance this was a false reading and she might not be pregnant. We had no choice but to wait for the official results. It felt like we were holding our breath for four days, waiting to exhale on Monday.

To complicate the situation even more, my grandparents had made the 6+ hour drive up to spend Christmas with our family, planning to leave on Sunday. We had to convince them to stay without giving them a good reason why, because if it turned out Vicky wasn't pregnant, we didn't want to upset them. (Note: convincing someone to stay without a reason why is never easy.) In the end, I enlisted the help of my mother.

I told her what was happening and how we didn't want to say anything in case it wasn't good news, but we wanted them present in person if there *was* an announcement to make. I still don't know exactly what she told them, but they stayed.

On Monday, December 27th, my wife had to work while I was off and fidgeting at my parent's house, praying and waiting. My grandparents were a bit on edge, having been convinced to stay for not just the one day, but *two*, since we wouldn't find out until late afternoon. Every time the house phone rang my mother jumped right alongside me. When it wasn't Vicky, she was always quick to get whomever it was off of the phone ASAP.

Looking back, everyone probably knew what we were waiting for. The plan was for Vicky to get off work, find out the results, call me with the results and then drive to my parent's house (about an hour from our apartment) and, if the news was good, we would announce it together.

I still vividly remember the call.

I stood in my parent's dining room where the phone was. I could barely contain myself as I braced for the result, but honestly, I was going to be super disappointed if we weren't pregnant. I held my breath as I got on the phone and heard Vicky's voice.

"I'm pregnant!"

Those were some of the sweetest words I'd ever heard, and coming from the one I loved was a very special moment for me. A smile the size of the Grand Canyon spread across my face. My mother walked over to the kitchen and saw the smile cross my face, which I quickly tried to hide. She let out a tiny gasp of joy as she attempted to conceal her own huge smile.

About an hour later, Vicky arrived and we announced to our entire family (*parents, brother, and grandparents*): **we were going to have a baby**. Everyone was excited for us. Of course, we weren't out of the woods just yet. Vicky had become pregnant, which was a miracle in itself. Now we had to work closely with the doctor to take this baby to term and deliver a happy healthy child. This meant constant monitoring by the doctor, as well as lots of sonograms, urine tests, blood work, and a bunch of other tests to ensure success. It was simultaneously a joyful and super stressful time.

If I thought I felt useless before, I *really* did during the entire first trimester. Vicky didn't have morning sickness or evening sickness, though. No, instead her body opted for the complete package of all-day sickness. It was so bad the doctor became concerned she wasn't getting enough nutrients for the baby and had her sucking on ice pops and eating as many pretzels as her stomach would allow.

He did mention to me once that it might be a result of the PCOD, but there was no way to be sure. For me this translated to my being totally and completely useless. Actually, there were a few times I was even *less* than useless, simply by being in the way.

I would try and help. I stroked her head or scratched her back, things which provided relief sometimes, but only made her feel worse other times. The problem was there was no way to decipher whether my efforts would be welcome or rejected until I tried, so there was always a risk involved.

I found myself sitting in the living room praying her pain and discomfort would stop. Almost like clockwork, as soon as we entered the second trimester her sickness ended. It was as if a switch had been turned off. I was so extremely happy, I didn't question it, going with the flow.

When I talk to young fathers-to-be these days, I tell them they'd better soak up the second trimester, because it's the best thing ever. During the second trimester the baby begins to move, the heartbeat is strong, a sonogram can show you your child, and your wife is super, super happy. She has that glow pregnant woman get.

It's a magical time for her, and she begins to show and everyone is excited for her and the new life growing inside. A new life which came about all because of you — the Dad to be. You made her pregnant. You are the man. In fact, you're kind of a Superman.

While everyone's rubbing your wife's belly and laughing, other fathers are high-fiving you and patting you on the back, all while a growing smirk forms on their faces. Sure, you think it's because you had sex, but the reality is they know what's coming and how unprepared you are. So they still slap you and stand with you and grin, knowing you only have a few short months to suck up all this adulation. Soon enough the third trimester will hit, and then all bets will be off.

For Vicky the third trimester arrived with a roar. She could no longer get comfortable on our bed. None of her clothes fit. She suddenly looked at herself in the mirror and felt fat. Understand that the previous day she was the same size and glowing with a cute belly. That day had come and gone. Today it wasn't anything but fat.

And in her third trimester mind, because she was fat meant there was no possible way I could still be in love with her. This list went on and on and on. I could do nothing right. If I rubbed her it was too much. If I didn't rub her, it was because I didn't find her attractive. If I complimented her, I didn't mean it or I was just saying that because I was "stuck" being married. If I tried to help by carrying things for her, I suddenly had no faith in her ability to be independent.

Ladies and gentlemen, it was a dark, dark time where I fondly reminisced the glory days of the second trimester. Still, I looked forward to the baby's arrival, a new life about to be added to our family. We thought we were doing okay, basically ready for what lie ahead of us. I can tell you, without a shadow of a doubt, we weren't close to being ready. We were on the other side of the *planet* from ready. Still, we continued to coast in our hopeful approach to the runway.

I was never a fan of Biology in High School, primarily because all the names were way too long and I was dyslexic. But I want to take a moment to define a couple of things for you so you can understand what was happening inside her. (*If you're a medical professional, feel free to skip ahead…*) Before a baby can be birthed naturally, there are a series of things the woman's body goes through toward the end of the pregnancy. All of these must be done before any pushing can happen (or at least before it's safe to push).

The first thing to know is the baby's due date is really a window of time. They give you a single date (like September 1st), but this really represents a window of about five weeks, starting three weeks before the due date and ending two weeks after. They'd like you to give birth during this window of time because it's ideal for all involved. Before three weeks is too early and the baby might not have fully developed. Too late, and there are issues for the mother.

Next important item is the baby has to "drop." The uterus holds and nurtures the baby at stomach level during the majority of the pregnancy. However, the baby has to get down to where it comes out before it can actually come out. This is the "drop," as the woman's body will maneuver the baby from the stomach area down into her hips and between her pelvis in preparation for the delivery of the baby through the birth canal. This has a funny measurement I don't fully understand, but I do know it's called "Zero Station" when the baby's in place for birth.

Another important thing to happen is the cervix (a fancy name for the cork holding the baby inside the woman) has to begin to open or "dilate." This is measured in centimeters, and there are several key points along this stretching open. I don't know them all but I know a couple.

For example, they will typically not give you an epidural (a special kind of numbing drug given in the spine) if you're six centimeters dilated or greater. They will also not usually give it until you're at least two centimeters dilated. I'm unsure of the rest of the key points. Basically, the door has to open so the baby can come out.

The last thing also happens to the cervix (the cork) which will thin and soften or "efface" so the baby can come out. Effacement is measured in percent, and they are ideally looking for full, or 100%, effacement for birth.

To wrap this up, for a baby to be born naturally, the baby has to be at zero station, the cervix has to be ten centimeters dilated and the cervix has to be at one hundred percent effacement. Only *then* can the woman begin pushing the baby out of the birth canal. There are tons of other things that can or do happen around the pregnancy, including some really bad things, but these were the ones that I remembered the most.

Six weeks before our due date, Vicky and I were at the doctor's office and he discovered she was two centimeters dilated and around 15% effaced. The baby wasn't at zero station and there was great concern about it being too early. So the doctor ordered my wife to go on complete bedrest. She could go to the bathroom and to the living room to lay on the couch, and that was it. He wanted to at least get within three weeks of the due date to let the baby "cook" some more, because a premature baby can have a lot of issues he wanted us to avoid.

So Vicky went on strict bedrest, which she didn't really appreciate. This also interrupted our attending of Lamaze class —where they teach soon-to-be parents all about the delivery process. We started classes about two months before our due date, figuring we had plenty of time. Instead, we were on bedrest after just one class, unable to attend the rest. This freaked me out, but I knew God was in control and tried really hard to just be there for Vicky.

If you know Vicky, then you know she *really* does not like being idle. She wasn't a big television watcher at the time, and it didn't help that we only had five channels for her to choose from, and definitely no on-demand or streaming options. Her choices were extremely limited, to put it mildly, and most days there was nothing on that she wanted to watch.

This meant her bedrest time was *driving her crazy*, and she would eagerly throw me in the backseat to take me along for the ride. I tried really hard to both help Vicky and remind her she had to keep laying down and resting. However, I had to go to work every day, which left Vicky alone several hours, laying there with essentially nothing to do.

Today, you have all of your streaming services and a ton of shows to watch or catch up on, and if that doesn't please you, there's an endless supply of movies. Back then, however, you had far less options. Daytime television consisted of soap operas and talk shows. To make things worse, I'd taken the doctor's concern for my wife's bed rest to heart. I had an image that if she moved too much, *BAM!* — the baby would suddenly drop out of her. (Give me some grace, it was my first child and I didn't know any better.) But it was on my mind *every single time* my wife decided to get up, so I was hyper-diligent about reminding her to lay back down.

Three long, tiring, drudging weeks clicked by at a snail's pace, but we managed to keep it together and not kill each other or *BAM!* — drop a baby into our living room. I was happy, blissfully thinking the hard part was over.

Boy, was I wrong.

We hadn't come *close* to the hard part.

On Tuesday, August 9th, 1994, we returned to our doctor's office. There we discovered my wife's body was now six centimeters dilated (*which meant they wouldn't give her an epidural*), the baby had dropped to zero station, and she was around thirty percent effaced. The doctor was super happy with us, and decided we were in the green zone and could start birthing a baby.

We were *beyond* excited.

The doctor ordered I take my wife to the mall, being indoors with ample air conditioning, and have her walk until her contractions started, aiming for five minutes apart at most. I was excited. *This* was something I could do, something I could finally *succeed* at. Take my wife to the mall? Could do. We love the mall anyway. Take her for a walk. Easy peasy. I mean, how hard could that be, right? She'd already walked into the doctor's office. Get those contractions going, down to five minutes apart? Piece of cake.

We were off to the races.

But first, allow me to set the scene.

The mall wasn't very crowded, as this was the middle of the day. I also worked at the mall, so I was intimately familiar with how it was laid out. I parked the car, we entered the mall and began walking.

It was nice. We were window shopping, chatting with a few people who knew us about how we were going to have a baby soon and were walking it out. It was a great time, almost too good to be true.

And then it happened.

My wife felt something.

Immediately I began timing, because this must be a contraction, right? She stopped for a second with kind of an "oh my," and then it passed. Finished as fast as it had begun. *Well, that was easy*, I thought. *Why do they show people screaming in the movies during these things? That was just cute little hiccup. No sweat. This is going to be so easy.*

(Cue the ominous musical score here…)

We'd been walking for about a half hour when the first *real* contraction hit. Vicky suddenly stopped, doubled over and screamed. This wasn't a half-second "oh my," but lasted more than twenty seconds. The entire time I'm trying to keep her walking, of course, because "the doctor told me to keep her walking."

She wasn't having any of that. She was in pain and wanted to sit.

"Remember what the doctor said," I gently reminded her.

"I don't care."

I happily encouraged her how millions of women just like her had given birth that month, and soon she would too, because she was the strongest person I knew. This didn't necessarily inspire her with confidence or strength, but I suppose it managed to keep her going.

Once the contraction was over, I began the timer. Ten minutes later the second hit. It was a touch worse, but we did our best to keep moving. The next one was slightly closer, and the pattern continued.

Now, I don't know if you've ever had to keep a screaming woman, writhing in obvious pain, walking in a semi-crowded public place, but let me just tell you: it's not easy. Not only did I have to deal with the anguish my wife was experiencing, but I also had to contend with onlookers who thought it was their job to inform me how cruel I was, "making this poor woman walk, and with child, no less." Some asked how I could be so barbaric, ignoring me when I explained it was "doctor's orders," and we were simply trying to get her contractions going.

Nothing I said made a difference. What was even more shocking was how I was being dressed down by older women, women who had presumably *had* children and should have known what was happening. Fortunately, there was a ray of hope. One of the ladies who worked in a store close to where I worked was also pregnant and had been in our Lamaze class. It wasn't her first child, and she was rooting us on. Every time we passed, even if there were people in her store, she would shout her encouragement to keep going. I can't tell you how encouraging that was for both of us. We almost wanted to speed up as we walked around, just to get back to her encouraging words.

Eight hours of walking later...

Vicky still wasn't at a point where the contractions were close enough to take her back to the hospital. It was almost seven in the evening, and all of my wife's amazing strength had left her. There was nothing left in the tank, and she told me we had to stop.

We went home, knowing the doctor was expecting her to be ready in a couple of hours in the delivery room. We felt it was safe to go home and rest, but it also made us wonder, after so many hours of physical exhaustion, what still lay ahead of us before we would see our baby.

I should note we'd decided to not discover the sex of our baby beforehand, something we did for all three of our children. We wanted those magical moments just after a child is born when the doctor declares what we had. We didn't know the sex of any of our children, and let me tell you, those crucial moments of revelation are among the ones I will most cherish for all eternity.

So we didn't check the sex, which upset everyone in the extended family. They were convinced we knew but were just not telling anyone. *Why would anyone do that?* I thought. That'd just be cruel.

The next morning we got a call from the doctor's office, surprised they hadn't heard about a new delivery. Our doctor was concerned. He asked if we were still walking. I jokingly said, "Absolutely, I just toss Vicky a sandwich every now and then!" He got the joke. However, his orders were the same: get to the mall and walk and walk and *walk* until the contractions were under five minutes apart.

So we psyched ourselves up and headed back to the mall. Many of the same people who had scolded us the day before were there, so we received many of the same comments. However, our friend was *also* there, encouraging us once more. We also had one of my co-workers, Ingrid, who had kind of adopted Vicky and I, like a cool aunt. Ingrid was super supportive, totally cheering us on. After so much exhaustion and discouragement, it was really nice to have this level of support.

One lap of the mall, and we were in the target zone and off to the hospital!

We wish. Instead, we got a couple of hours in before we were finally under the five-minute mark. We told everyone we were on our way to the hospital and made our way to the car. Everything was going great. We raced five minutes down the road and entered the hospital... at which point Vicky mentions to me the contractions had stopped.

A flood of emotions washed over me. I *really* didn't want to go back to the mall and walk again. I was tired, Vicky was exhausted, and I was pretty sure neither of us could take another couple of hours of walking. Instead, we decided to go up to the labor and delivery floor and check in to let them know what was happening.

The nurses set us up in a room and called our doctor, who was quick to arrive as his office was connected to the hospital. Vicky's last contraction was at the mall and the doctor assessed the situation. He decided that instead of walking some more he was going to give Vicky

Pitocin, a drug to help kick things along. We were relieved, exhausted, excited, tired, and thinking we were totally ready for the arrival of our first born.

Remember the Lamaze class we attended one session of? Well, during the class you learn a lot of valuable information about what to expect, what drugs are available, what different tools might be used, what some of the terms are, and various ways to help you mitigate the pain — which doesn't work, in my opinion. One of the last things that class does is tour the labor and delivery floor of the hospital, showing the expectant parents what the room looks like so they aren't surprised.

Any guesses which night they happened to pick to tour the delivery floor?

That's right. The class we attended for all of one session was touring the labor floor *at the exact moment* Vicky was juiced up and feeling some major contractions at about two minutes apart. The class quickly looked in on us, but didn't stay long. Instead, they moved on to show the other parents-to-be an empty room.

Did I mention the drug Pitocin and how it works? The drug's designed to help the woman's body kickstart contractions. In my mind, this meant we would slowly have a mild contraction (one of the "oh my" ones) around every five minutes apart. Then over the course of, say, a few hours, slowly bring us up to speed at a contraction every two minutes.

I couldn't have been more wrong.

Instead, Pitocin takes you from zero to one hundred and sixty in a matter of *seconds*. The first contraction to hit after Vicky was dosed was a hard one. Let me pause here and let everyone who have not had a child or been in labor and delivery room when a child is on the way — you have *no idea* the level of excruciating pain a contraction will be.

Imagine the worst pain you've ever experienced and multiply that by a hundred. Then double it, and add four more, for good measure. Then double it *again*, and you'll begin to get close.

We were totally unprepared for the level of pain Vicky was experiencing. The thing about my wife is she's the strongest person that I know. She can bear anything, survive anything, and always finds a way, never failing. She just doesn't know *how* to fail. This woman could have a semi-truck roll over her and she'd still get up and go to work. But that day she was suddenly having trouble breathing because of how intense the pain was.

We arrived at the hospital around noon, but it was probably around 1pm that the Pitocin started working. It took several hours (eight?) before my wife's body was ready. Remember, she came in at six centimeters dilated, with only four to go. She wasn't quite half effaced and the baby had dropped. All indicators in my mind pointed to a quick delivery.

Not at all.

However, the worst part for me was yet to come.

Tuesday, August 9th, the day before, we had a sonogram done to see how our child was doing. Everything was perfect. The baby was where it was supposed to be and ready to see the world, my wife was ready to see the child who had been growing inside her, and I was ready to move to the next phase of this journey. Back at the hospital, doctor declared everything was right and it was time to push.

This is where the woman will literally push the baby out of her uterus through the birth canal into the world. For a first-time birth, it can take a long time. An hour and half later the baby crowned, meaning the top of the head was visible, and he was called back in the room. The nurses stationed themselves around the bed as the doctor took command and began giving orders.

It was all flowing in a rhythm and soon we would see our baby. Then the doctor's face dropped. He uttered something I couldn't make out, and the whole room became electrified, everyone shifting into crisis mode. The nurse closest to me shoved me out of the way and literally hopped up on top of my wife's stomach. She was doing something that I couldn't make out. The doctor, usually full of joy and smiling and cracking jokes, had a stern and serious look on his face.

I knew then something was wrong.

Something was very wrong.

Understand me when I say I don't mean to diminish the journey my wife was in any way. But when I was shoved back out of the way, I knew something serious was happening. I didn't know what, but my mind was filling in the blanks. I imagined a vivid scene, witnessing the loss of both my coming child and my wife. On top of that was the horror that there was absolutely nothing I could do. I couldn't fix something or break something or cut something or mend something or shout something or do a blessed thing.

All I could do was stand there and watch. Watch and be completely useless. It seemed like an eternity before the nurse climbed down off my wife, and I died a thousands deaths in that moment of helplessness.

What happened was our baby decided it wasn't comfortable, turning suddenly to face *sideways*. Why is this an issue? In the ideal setting, the baby will be face down as the woman lays upright giving birth. This is to allow for quick evacuation of any of the amniotic fluid in the baby just a little bit before keeping it alive. This has to be done quickly, because at the moment of birth the baby isn't breathing, so someone has to open the passageways for the baby to breath. This is why doctors want to hear the baby cry, to know they were able get air into their lungs and draw a full breath.

However, there is a second reason a baby's ideal delivery is face down, and that's all about the shoulders. The baby's shoulders are left to right, spanning the woman's body, positioned perfectly to pass through the pelvis bones and come into the word. If the baby is turned to the left or right, at a certain point the shoulders will not be able to pass through the pelvis and the baby will become stuck. When this happens, the doctor will quickly notify a trained nurse to get on top of the woman and massage her belly, forcing the baby's shoulders into the *correct* position and turning it so it can be born.

This is what happened to our child, why I was pushed out of the way. They had mere minutes to get the baby turned, birthed, and the airways cleared to avoid any potential brain damage. This is why everyone became so serious, so fast. This wasn't normal, and I had no training about what needed to happen and they certainly didn't have time to explain it to me. After it was over, I was thankful they knew what they were doing.

With the crisis averted and the nurse climbing back down, the focus shifted back to pushing. The doctor called me over to help with the remainder of the birth. I got to watch the miracle of life as it was happening. I was truly awe-inspiring, breathtaking. God totally knew what He was doing when He allowed us to bring new life into this world. I know it was longer, but it really only felt like two pushes before our baby was out and laying on the table.

It was at this point that the doctor called me over. He looked down at our beautiful baby girl and then up at me. "This is why I do what I do!" he said, handing me a pair of scissors and asking if I would cut the cord. I was about to ask what that meant when he held up the umbilical cord, motioning to where I should cut.

Honestly, we thought we were having a boy, only because the Aquilone's have a strong history of birthing boys. Going back several generations, the ratio was something like nine out of every ten were boys. So the odds were in strong favor of our having a boy, and our doctor had overheard us talking about this. When our daughter arrived and both the doctor and I could see it was clearly *not* a boy, we suddenly looked up at each other in synchronized, shocked surprise. I was totally taken aback. I had a daughter! And I couldn't have been more excited about it. But the initial hesitation and the looks on our faces alarmed Vicky.

"What is the matter?" she asked.

The doctor turned to her, grinning. "It's a girl!"

You could have heard a pin drop.

Once we cut the cord, the nurses started shouting out some numbers. They briefly laid our baby girl on Vicky's chest so she was able to see her new daughter. There's nothing like the moment when the doctor announces "It's a girl!", but I tell you, there what's even more precious is when a woman who's just given birth looks into the face of her new born child.

We weren't out of the woods yet, however. The nurses took our daughter to be weighed and had shouted out a number I would later learn was an APGAR — a rating on the health of the baby, based on some key checks. This brought renewed concern into the room, and they immediately took our baby out.

I don't remember exactly what they said when they were taking her, but we got the impression they were going to clean her up and bring her back. Only…that didn't happen. At some point, they returned to tell us our baby had a bad case of jaundice, and literally needed to be "cooked" a little longer under ultraviolet lights. I had no idea what this was about, and they didn't exactly do a great job of explaining it to us. Fortunately, one of our friends from church was a pediatrician, and soon explained what jaundice was.

She told us it wasn't unusual for babies to have jaundice, and that it was almost expected with early births. I wish I could tell you her words made me feel better, but they didn't. Especially when going down and looking through the glass at my daughter, set off to the side from other kids, isolated in a plastic tube with lights over her. We were only allowed to take her out for feedings, and even then it wasn't nearly long enough.

It was grueling, looking at her under those lights. Especially when she would be crying. I wanted to punch some of the nurses for not picking her up or letting us hold her when she cried. Eventually the jaundice went away, though, and after several days my wife was discharged and we were finally able to take our baby home.

Katherine "Katie" Marie.

Named after my great uncle's wife and both of our grandmothers. It was a long journey to see her become part of our lives, and she was and remains one of the most amazing blessings in my life. I'm so proud of my daughter and the woman she's become. Super thankful to God that He had a different plan for us, sending us this doctor to help make it happen.

This stone is in my altar because it taught me how *nothing* is ever impossible with God. He'd used an amazing doctor to help navigate us through the twists and turns to the final blessing God had ordained to give us. Any other doctor would have probably just written us off. In fact, over the years there have been other doctors who can't believe we even have children. Yet God is good, and this stone reminds me of it all the time. It also reminds me to stay resolutely focused on what God says to us, listening to His voice and ignoring all others. Because blessing comes from listening and following what God says.

TRACING A MIRACLE

'It shall come about, if you listen obediently to my commandments which I'm commanding you today, to love the Lord your God and to serve Him with all your heart and all your soul, that He will give the rain for your land in its season, the early and late rain, that you may gather in your grain and your new wine and your oil.'
- Deuteronomy 11:13-14

I believe it was March of 1995 when Vicky and I'd decided to take our tax return and purchase a new car. We'd been driving around in a Ford Escort (the first models they made) for some time, and it was really showing its age. We did get our fair share of the economy class model of cars, racking up over one hundred thousand miles and still chugging along, a feat that shocked the junkyard dealer when we called him to sell him what was left of the car.

He gave me a low price and asked, "Where do I pick it up?" I told him I could drive it down to him, and he responded with, "It still drives??? Tell you what, I'll double my price if you can drive it to me!"

So I did and he did. It was still a small amount, but it was *something* and we knew it didn't have a lot of life left in it. I would've felt bad if we'd sold it someone else and it died before they got their money's worth.

We coupled the few hundred dollars from that sale with our tax return and wound up with a whopping fifteen hundred dollars. Now, I'm getting up there in years and as of today, fifteen hundred won't even pay the taxes on a new car. However, back then it might have made a decent payment on a good used car. (Most likely not a new car.) But we weren't picky, we just wanted a reliable car. We had one child with another on the way *(spoiler, oops)*, so we began looking to see what might be available.

I reached out and spoke with my grandfather for tips on buying cars, since he had purchased a lot of cars over the years. I'd thought if I got his wisdom and then spoke with my father and gained *his* wisdom, I would be in a good place to attempt to purchase my very first car. However, that wasn't in the cards, as I never spoke to my dad to ask him for tips.

Instead, my grandfather offered to co-buy the car with me. This meant that he would basically purchase the car, I would give him my down payment and make monthly payments to him. This sounded legit, and I was excited about getting a new car.

At the same time, there was an elder in the church we attended in upstate New York who discipled me in Christ and was one of my spiritual fathers. His day job was being a mechanic in the Air Force, working on ground vehicles and keeping them running. He was very good at his job. So it happened he was selling an older car he'd been keeping in fairly good shape. The car was a 1979 Pontiac Lemans. It burned through oil, but otherwise was in good shape.

The elder assured me that the oil burning issue was a minor issue, but if I didn't put a quart of oil in the car almost every day then it would become a major issue. He was asking fifteen hundred dollars for the car, the exact amount of money we had on hand.

Faced with two options to spend our money on, we did what any brand new Christian would do — we prayed and sought additional counsel. The other leaders of the church had encouraged us to not go into debt, aware of our financial situation. This was great advice, and one we should have listened too. However, the choice was purchasing a small, battered and weathered dingy or a brand new, shiny, thirty-five foot speedboat. Obviously God would want me to have the shiny one and not the beat up one, right? I mean, it would look good on God if his people were driving around in the latest and greatest cars, not to mention the people that would flock to the church where the blessings were flowing so openly. Right? *Right?!*

While I was praying, I knew God was speaking to me about buying the Lemans from the elder of my church. But...I didn't *want* the Lemans. It wasn't a happy color. It didn't have any new or fancy dashboard accoutrements. The radio was ancient. And the seats were... exceptionally used. However, God kept speaking to me to purchase this car.

So I did what any born again, blood-bought, spirit-filled baby Christian would have done. I called the elder and told him, "I'm sorry, but God told me to buy the new car."

He was gracious with me and encouraged me that there would be no hard feelings. He did suggest that it wasn't a good idea, but he wouldn't stand in my way of following what God had spoken to me. That last part should have stung, but I was so enamored by the idea of the new car I'm sorry to say it fell on deaf ears. I hung up the phone and immediately notified my grandfather to go ahead with the purchase.

On Monday, February 13th, 1995, I received a call from my grand-father. The 1995 Mercury Tracer had been bought and was sitting in his driveway. All we needed to do was to come and get it. Which wasn't an easy feat, since my grandfather lived some three hundred miles away, back when the speed limit on highways was fifty-five. To add to this, we lived in very upstate New York. If you were to draw a line straight north from New York City until you hit the Canadian border and came back directly south about fifty miles, you would find a town called Plattsburgh. This is where we lived, and there were no major airports there. The closest airport would have been Burlington, across Lake Champlain. However, back then it was a very small airport and flights weren't cheap.

Tuesday February 14th, 1995. Valentine's Day. We had spoken with some friends who agreed to drive us to Albany where my grandfather would meet and take us the rest of the way. We pulled into my grandfather's driveway very late in the day, but super excited about the new car. It was bigger than the Escort and had better gas mileage. Since it was new, it was far more reliable and wouldn't need to have as much money sunk into repairs.

We couldn't have been happier.

Well, we thought so, at least. There was a still, small voice nagging in the back of my mind that I was doing my absolute best to ignore.

Wednesday February 15th, we made the six-hour drive back home. The car performed great over the long drive, that small voice was getting easier and easier to push away.

It was a done deal. Money had changed hands and the vehicle was ours. All that was left was to enjoy the car and make the payments. Oh, and make those really, really high insurance payments, seeing as how it was a brand new car and needed comprehensive and collision, as well as the basics. In addition I'd just turned twenty five and had a few scraps on our records. But I was driving a new car, smiling and happy.

Saturday February 18th, just before President's Day and a holiday weekend, we decided to drive to Vicky's side of our family and show them the new car. They lived about one hundred and fifty miles from us at the time, on the southern side of the Adirondack mountains and about forty-five minutes northwest of Albany. It felt good to show them the car that "we" had bought. It felt very grown up. It felt like we were showing them we had finally "arrived" as adults, now that we had a kid and a car.

While showing off the car, we decided to go out and eat lunch at the local Ponderosa restaurant. It was a favorite of ours, since you could order a steak and have a buffet of many other items. The one near Vicky's side of the family had the super buffet, which had a ton more items to select from. It was an experience, for sure.

When we drove to the restaurant in our new car, Vicky's sister sat in the back seat, pressed between Katie's car seat and the passenger side door. It was a tight fit, but she had somehow managed it. So while we were dining, we discussed moving Katie's car seat directly behind my seat to give Vicky's sister more room on the ride back. We all agreed it was a great idea, and we would've done just that, if it hadn't started to drizzle. Racing to the car in an attempt to avoid getting wet, we completely forgot about moving the seat, piled in and off we went.

I was looking for a Christian bookstore that I'd seen in the Yellow Pages — the old giant book that listed everyone's and every business's phone number and address. However, I wasn't able to find this elusive store, no matter how many times I went up and down the street. Many months later I would find the store and walk around it, but on this day, that fateful Saturday in February, I couldn't find it.

I'd just about given up when we approached an intersection. It was a normal intersection with a stoplight that, to this day, I sincerely believe was green when I glanced at it. That's what I remember, but apparently I was completely wrong. According to several eyewitnesses, the light in my direction was not only red, but had been red for some time when I went careening into the middle of the crossroad.

Everything slowed down, almost like I was caught in Bullet Time in the movie *The Matrix*, except I'd slowed down as well. I saw the car slowly moving into the center of the intersection. It seemed so clear.

Suddenly there was a sound of clashing swords, only much, *much* louder, followed by the sound of bending or warping metal. I began to turn my head toward my left side as the twisting metal clashed with the new sound of shattering glass. We were no longer moving forward, but sliding right, toward the opposite corner of the intersection. We had been hit, and were slowly coming to a stop.

All I could do was watch.

The accident occurred because as I was about halfway through the intersection, directly under the hanging stoplight, a very large, old tank of a Chevy truck came barreling down from my left. It broadsided our brand new car. There wasn't anything the other driver could do. They'd been going the speed limit, and a building made it difficult to not only see me, but notice I wasn't stopping. By the time the driver came to the realization and hit the brakes, it was too late.

Well, too avoid a collision, but definitely just in time to save our lives. According to the police officer later, had they *not* hit the brakes, there was a very good chance it would have rolled over the top of our car, completely crushing the seating compartment under the weight.

The car was totaled that day, but our lives were saved, and I thank God for the other driver's quick reflexes and reaction time.

Once our car came to a stop, my emergency mode kicked in and I immediately began to assess what needed to be done. First, turn off the car, in case of a gas line break. Second, look around me, making a quick assessment to see if anyone was in dire need of medical attention. I didn't see any blood or anything else that appeared serious. There were no cell phones back then, so there was no calling for emergency services

Next up was to assess myself. However, this was quickly interrupted by my wife, darting out of the car to get to her sister and our daughter. Vicky's sister was quickly unbuckling Katie from the car seat and Katie was now screaming. They took her about twenty feet away and started to look her over, flipping her face down to allow for any glass that may have gotten in her mouth to fall out before she could swallow. At this point, some of the witnesses were coming to my wife's aid.

I heard sirens in the distance. I knew that I wasn't going out the driver's side door, as there was now a Chevy pushed up against it. I did a visual check of my body to see if there was blood or anything protruding out that shouldn't be. Thank God, there wasn't. Still, I needed to get out, and that was where I had a problem. My obesity wasn't the problem — the problem was the driver's side door had become pushed in so much that I was now pinned between it and the center console.

Immediately every movie and TV car crash I'd ever seen came to mind. You know the ones where inevitably the car explodes? That's what played on the screen of my imagination. I started to panic, then mentally slapped myself and resolved to get out of the car. I was pinned pretty good, but was eventually able to push through quite a bit of pain and wiggle my way out of the car, joining my wife and sister-in-law in the middle of the road.

At this point, the paramedics arrived and tried to assess Katie's injuries, but Vicky wasn't ready to give up her daughter just yet. The medics were very professional, however, working around the concerned new mother until she was comforted that her daughter was in good hands. They determined Katie had, seconds before the crash, looked toward the truck, because there was only glass on her right side, the car seat completely shielding her left side.

They were still concerned that she might have swallowed some glass, and decided she needed to be rushed to the hospital. Vicky, her sister and my daughter piled into the ambulance and were off. I'd asked if I could go, but the paramedics explained there wasn't enough room and I still needed to give a statement to the police.

Ironically, I now stood in the middle of the intersection as the flat bed tow truck pulled away. A police officer asked me what happened, and I told him the truth. I thought the light was green, but witnesses said it was red. The truck hit me, so I must have been wrong.

I don't remember if he gave me a ticket. I *do* remember he gave me information about where my car was being taken. I also remember he was about to get in his car and leave when I asked him a question.

"Um how do I get to the hospital?"

He frowned and said "I could call someone or maybe a taxi. I thought you were going ride with the tow truck."

The tow truck, to my understanding, wasn't going to the hospital. I explained how I didn't know my in-law's numbers to call, and really had no other way to get to the hospital. After some internal debate, he somewhat reluctantly decided to take me. It was an awkwardly silent, long ride to the hospital.

Bursting into the emergency room where my wife and Katie were, I could finally breathe a sigh of relief. They determined Katie hadn't swallowed any glass, and didn't even have any cuts. Somehow the glass had hit her and settled on her skin, but not injure her one bit. Thank God!!

This is when my wife revealed a piece of information that shocked me to my core, just about dropping me to my knees. "You realize that God protected Katie," she began, "because if we had remembered to move the car seat, the front bumper of the truck would have crushed her." The truck had pushed in the rear door all the way up to her seat, even dislodging the car seat, but didn't hurt our little girl.

The paramedics explained what would have happened had we not moved her, because they had seen it all too often. One would think that the crushing and pushing metal would have just pushed the car seat over. However, they said what would have happened in our car was as the truck bent the driver's side rear door toward the car seat, the seatbelts would have locked to keep the car seat secure. This would have pinned the car seat under the large amounts of metal, crushing her. Katie would have had all the weight of a Chevy truck bumper *plus* the metal from the driver's side of the car.

She would have died.

I will never be able to thank God enough for saving our little girl that day.

Our weekend trip wound up being extended, as we had to wait until Tuesday to get an insurance adjuster out to see the car. Unsurprisingly, it was declared as totaled. Because we had like a total of six hundred miles on the car, however, they gave us back the entire purchase amount, and within weeks I received in my hand a check for fifteen hundred dollars.

My grandfather informed me that they had several other Tracers on the lot, so he could get us another one and work out how to get it to us. As much as I appreciated my grandfather's offer, I knew that I *knew* that I wasn't supposed to buy the new car. My small voice had become a roaring lion, one that was telling me to purchase the car from the elder and *not* go into debt. It was telling me to trust in God, and He would take care of us.

The next day I called up the elder and asked if he was still selling the car. He was, and soon after I bought the 1979 Pontiac Lemans. We had to put oil in it every day, but it never failed to get us where we needed to go. It turned out to be an absolute blessing of a vehicle for us, and all because I finally listened to God.

This stone is in my altar because it encourages me to always listen to God's voice — even when I don't want to or if what He's saying doesn't seem to make sense. God will always have our back and always speak to us about what is the best thing for us.

That car was a blessing every day we had it. In fact, a few days after giving it away, we heard it threw a rod and was totaled. (Fortunately, no one was hurt.) This also taught me that even when you fail to follow God's voice, you never completely walk out from under God's protection.

We could have all died or lost our miracle child or who knows what other possible outcomes could have happened. Instead, God put His hands around us, and outside of some bruises on my hip, we walked out unharmed. Thank you, God!!

GOD IS THE BEST TEST TAKER

'But if any of you lacks wisdom, let him ask of God, who gives to all generously and without reproach, and it will be given to him.'
- James 1:5

After finishing community college, Vicky and I discussed what we should do next. There were really two options. First, return to the local four-year college where I had attended and flunked out, because I didn't apply myself. Second, I could look for a college somewhere else. It was a difficult decision, because the local college and the local area of upstate New York was familiar to us. It was where we met and began our family, where two of our eventual three children were born. Returning to our comfort zone was the clear answer.

However, we prayed a lot and decided God not only wanted me to continue my education, but He wanted us to move to a new area — a new adventure. Honestly, it was a bit terrifying, yet God never left our side. While praying one day, I felt He was directing me to go for an engineering degree, partially because I always loved math, science and computers, but also because God opened the door for me to go to Rutgers University.

Rutgers is part of the state university system of New Jersey. I was born in New Jersey, Denville, but also lived in Mount Arlington, Sicklerville, Lincoln Park and Pequannock. This was all before I was fifteen, when my parents made the move to upstate New York. They felt the living conditions would be better in a more rural area than in the middle of the suburbs.

Now, at the age of 26, my wife and I were moving back to New Jersey, into a small, low-rent complex called Somerset Estates in Franklin Township. This would be a new area (central Jersey), as opposed to having lived in north (Pequannock, Lincoln Park) and south (Sicklerville) Jersey in the past. We would still be a good ninety minute drive from any family members (assuming traffic was favorable), making it feel as if we'd moved into a place where we knew no one. However, we felt God was with us, and we were excited.

When I first stepped onto the campus, I had a confidence and peace, knowing God was with me. I knew the classes would be harder, though, and there would be challenges ahead. As long as I remained close to God, He would see me through it all.

Thankfully a ton of my community college credits transferred over, so all of my basic classes were out of the way. All that was left were some core classes, plus some extra math and science. In fact, my first semester was a math class, a physics class (which I loved), a computer science class and my first electrical engineering class. No English or History in sight as those requirements were previously filled, to my relief.

At the end of my first semester, I had four three-hour finals in a twenty-seven hour period. According to the school policies regarding finals, this was considered too much for one person and one of my professors would have to move their exam or make a special accommodation for me. However, upon speaking with each of my professors about the issue, they all had the same response. "Have one of your other professors accommodate you!"

I attempted a second round of discussion with the professors, this time explaining that none of the others would help (despite the policy), but none of them budged. At this point, I had two options. First, I could go to the dean and force a professor to do something. I felt that would cause a lot of problems for me in the future, not to mention potentially affect my current grade. (It's not supposed to, of course, but then, they were supposed to be more helpful with my finals schedule to begin with, and you see how far that got me).

Second option? I could bite the bullet and just take the exams as they were laid out. As God would have it, I'd met some amazingly great people (*I'm looking at you two, Geoff and Dave*) who had the same classes and exams. We quickly formed a study group. We pulled an all-nighter getting ready for the first day's exams, at 11:30am and 3pm. Trying desperately to cram everything in, we pulled a second all-nighter studying for the final two exams, at 8am and 11:30am the next day.

Yes, you read that right.

We pulled two back-to-back all-nighters to study for our finals, because we were determined to ace each one.

So I'd been up for something like fifty-two hours straight when I headed into my last final exam. Math. Differential Equations, more affectionally known as "Diffy-Q." I'd figured since math always came easy to me, despite it being a higher-level course, I should be able to still pull off a good grade. However, when I was in college this second time around, I was insanely set on getting good grades — all A's, if possible. Pulling the second all-nighter seemed like the logical choice to help me nail both second day finals.

I was wrong.

Really, *really* wrong.

Here's what I remember:

I remember walking into the classroom and sitting down. I remember watching the exam booklets being passed out, and hearing the instructions. I remember writing my name down. I also remember thinking how dead tired I was and hoping I'd to be able to focus. I remember saying a prayer of some sort, but not the contents of the prayer.

And then…I remember the professor announcing our time was

up. All exam booklets were passed down the aisles and he began collecting exams.

Instantly I panicked.

I didn't remember a blessed thing after writing my name down. Sudden realization hit me: I must have fallen asleep and completely and royally screwed up my final. I quickly opened the booklet. I had in my head that if I could scribble something down — *anything* — it somehow wouldn't be as bad and turning in absolutely nothing.

I was desperate. If I tried my best and failed, I could accept that. If it turned out that all I knew was only worth a failing grade, I could live with that. I would deal with it and figure out what to do next. But to fail because I fell asleep and not even answer a single question was unacceptable.

I needed to do *something*!

I opened the booklet. Shock flooded my body, cold shivers shooting up and down my spine. I couldn't believe my eyes.

The exam booklet had writing in it.

Not just any writing, mind you, but math — the kind that looked like it belonged in this class. I was utterly confused, scrambling to see what was written as the professor arrived at my row. I looked up at him, and he extended his hand, waiting. Sighing, I handed him the unfinished booklet, only then noticing there was writing from front to back. Not one page I saw had been missed, although I couldn't make out if it was right or not.

Here's the thing: I didn't take that exam. I was too exhausted, physically and mentally. Instead, I believe God took the exam for me. Or rather, *through* me. Understand, I'd been doing the work, putting in the time and studying. One could even argue I'd put in *too* much time studying. Yet when it came time for the actual exam, it was as if God said, "I got this for you!"

Of course, I'm not saying God will take an exam for you if you haven't done the work or studied. It's more likely He won't. (I shared this once as a speaker at school, and had a middle schooler approach me later, asking, "How can I make God take my exams?" He had missed the point.)

God took the exam for me because God is loving and compassionate and saw how exhausted I was, coupled with how hard I'd worked. Had I not studied and simply strolled into that exam, I'm sure I would have been on my own. (To this young kid's dismay, I informed him first off he needed to be a really good student.)

Do I *truly* I believe God took the exam for me? I do, and here's why. Math has always been my best subject, but this particular high-level math had been a serious struggle for me. No matter how hard I tried, I found the book confusing and the class even more confounding. I would do the homework and feel great about my work, until I compared what I got with the actual answers and saw they didn't match.

It was the oddest sensation for me as Math had always been pretty clear cut. In this class, though, I was struggling to pull off a high C, and even *that* was with a pretty significant curve. (Note: a curve on a grade is where the professor decides, usually due to the whole class's poor performance, to increase the given points or lower the break-points for where the letter grades would be. So an 80 might become an A).

A second reason is I pulled the all-nighters studying. A good grade on the final would have pushed me over the top to a solid B-. In the end, I received a B+ in the class. A B+! When I later checked on how that was possible, given my grades going into the final, I discovered I had *aced* the final.

I'd gotten every single answer right.

There is no way in my exhausted state this was possible. One might argue that I just don't remember taking it, because I was so tired. It's a valid point, but quickly falls apart when you compare my grades heading into the final with what I received on the final. Furthermore, when I spoke with a few of my fellow students about the exam, I quickly discovered I didn't even know *how* to answer a couple of the questions. I wanted to, but just couldn't do it! Honestly, there was simply no way I could have aced that exam.

This is a stone in my altar because it showed me that Jesus doesn't just walk by my side as a spectator. Instead He's an active participant in my life. Whether He is speaking aid or clearing a path or working a miracle or taking a test for you, God is always *deeply* involved in your life. Jesus didn't just walk with me that day; *He took the exam for me*.

Wherever you may be in life or whatever you've done in the past, commit today to follow after God and do what He tells you, and maybe, just maybe, the day will come when He will take a test *for* you.

I DON'T WANT NANA TO BE WITH JESUS

"'It will come about after this That I will pour out My Spirit on all mankind; And your sons and daughters will prophesy, Your old men will dream dreams, Your young men will see visions. '
- Joel 2:28

Christmas 1997 was a very special holiday for my family. For the first time in a very long time, our entire family gathered at my grandparent's house to celebrate. Even better? There were no fights that year.

No one stormed out mad or kept bringing up that one item that always sets another person off. No arguments. No raised voices. Nothing of the sort. We all got to enjoy each other and were actually one big, happy family. This was especially important to me, because at the time my parents lived about three hundred miles away and we rarely saw them. Couple that with the fact that our middle child, Abby, was six months old when we moved away, and we basically had very little interaction with my parents. If I'd known what was about to happen, I would have found a way to spend more time with them. But you always think you'll have more time with our loved ones than we do, and I was doing the best I could for my immediate family. Plus, I knew my parents wanted me to continue to pursue my bachelor's degree, even if it meant living so far away.

January 4th, 1998, was a typical Sunday for us. We'd attended church in the morning, followed by lunch with some of the church people we tended to hang around with. Home for a quick afternoon nap and then off to finish up with home group Bible study at one of the elder's homes where we had been attending for about a year or more.

Since I was on winter break from college, this was a time for us to regroup and refresh and feel a sense of relaxation before the chaos of the second semester began, which from all accounts promised to be very intense. On the way home from the group, Katie, our oldest, suddenly started crying. Immediately my wife, Vicky, turned around to try and assess the situation. "What's wrong?" she asked her.

"I don't want Nana to go be with Jesus!" Katie wailed.

Nana was the grandma name for my mother, and until that moment we thought she was in good health. I mean, we had just had a great Christmas and no one seemed ill, under the weather or out of sorts. Even my Dad, who had had several heart attacks (or strokes or cardiac infractions or whatever they were technically called) over the previous several years seemed in good health and spirits.

So when Katie mentioned my mother, I figured she was confused and was really concerned about my Dad / Poppa's health. We reassured her that Nana wasn't going to be with Jesus any time soon, but Katie was insistent that Jesus had told her Nana was going to be with Him soon, so we agreed we would call my parents when we got home.

Mom sounded a bit under the weather, but no more than anyone else would with a cold. I made sure to have Katie speak to her on the phone and have my mother assure her that she was fine. In fact, everyone got on the phone and spoke with my Mom, each of us telling her we loved her. We had a great talk, and before I hung up I made a point of telling my mother once more how much I loved her. Looking back, I think it was really more instinct than just being intentional. However, my Dad would later tell me that the call — and my specifically telling her I loved her — meant the world to her. If I knew that was the last conversation I would ever have with her, there would have been so much more I would have loved to talk about and tell her. None of it more important than saying I love you, of course. Just having more time to hear her voice, more time for my kiddos to grow up and get to know her.

Monday, January 5th, started like any other day. I'd gotten up and was kind of lounging around the house when the phone rang mid-afternoon. It was my grandmother, calling to tell me they thought my mother had a heart attack, and she was being rushed to the hospital. Immediately I assumed my grandmother had either got the wrong message or somehow messed up the message, because it was my *father* who had the heart condition, not Mom.

I thanked her and told her I would call the hospital and find out what was happening. Since I used to live in the area, I knew the only hospital where they could have taken my Dad.

I called the telephone operator to get the hospital phone number. I mentioned to the women on the phone that I was trying to find out what happened to my Dad, so instead of just giving me the number she immediately connected me.

The front desk answered the phone and I explained I was looking for an "Aquilone," having received the message that someone from my family had been rushed there. The attendant quickly replied, "Yes, an Aquilone arrived here just a little bit ago by ambulance." I asked if I could be connected to any family member who had come in with the ambulance, assuming it would be my Mom. The attendant grew somber. "I'll connect you to the family room."

My heart sank. I immediately understood the subtext, as the "family room" was a special area for grieving family members to gather after someone has passed. It was a place to console and say final goodbyes before the body was transported to the morgue. I mentally prepared to hear my Mom's voice, as I'd been preparing for a few years that any moment with my Dad might be his last. I realize today, as I write these words, that no matter how much you may think you're prepared, you're never truly ready for a parent's passing. Without a shadow of a doubt, I was totally unprepared for what happened next.

My father's voice spoke on the other end of the line. "Mom's gone!"

Time stopped. Breathing stopped.

The entire world stopped as I stood there, holding the phone, desperately waiting to hear this was some kind of joke — a cruel, horrible prank.

That never happened.

My Dad continued to speak, but his voice was slowed down and muffled. I lost all my strength and lowered myself, collapsing to the floor. As I leaned against the wall, I felt myself sink deeper and deeper into the floor. My heart slammed down into my stomach, where any second now I was going to throw it back up. I was in shock. Waves of tears ran down my face.

"Patrick!" my father shouted over the phone.

I'm sure he understood what I was going through, what we were all going through, and was trying to get my attention. It felt like an eternity before I was able to move again, gathering myself enough to continue. "What happened?" I asked.

He recounted how Mom had been sick, but it seemed like just an ordinary cold. She had called a doctor Sunday night, just before we had called her. Since they didn't have insurance, the doctor at the immediate care center subscribed her a prescription over the phone, without seeing or examining her. In the morning, she was sitting on the couch, nursing a cup of Constant Comment tea (a favorite Mom and I regularly shared). As my father came out from the bedroom, he noticed her legs had turned dark purple.

"Glenda," he said, "your legs!"

"I know," she replied, "and my tongue is swollen!"

My Dad announced they were going to the hospital. My Mom insisted on taking a shower and getting dressed. Dad told her to hurry, as the trip to the nearest hospital from where they lived in upstate New York was about forty minutes (at the posted speed limit, which I'm sure my Dad wouldn't have been doing). He called 911 in case the ambulance could get there before they were ready to take the car, and on the chance they could meet the ambulance en route, which was common in their rural area.

My father always regretted not throwing her in the car and leaving immediately. In truth, I doubt it would have changed anything but there was no convincing him of this. Honestly, there would be no convincing me, either. My parents had made it to the back porch on their way to the car when suddenly my mother stopped. "Oh," she said, and fell backwards into my Dad's arms. She had a smile on her face, and was gone the instant she hit his arms. Family and friends tried to comfort us later by telling us it was so quick she didn't suffer. Here one second and gone the next. The words might be true, but it definitely wasn't very comforting.

My Dad feverishly tried to revive her as the ambulance he had called earlier arrived and took over attempting to resuscitate her. One of the EMTs was a family friend, a best man at my brother's wedding. He knew she was gone, but they still tried everything they could. I believe the efforts were more for the sake of my father than any chance of bringing her back. They pronounced her dead on arrival at the hospital.

As my father finished, I told him I would be up as soon as I could pack the car and travel the almost seven-hour trip. He said he would see me soon and we hung up. I was crying as Vicky asked me what had happened. I tried to tell her, but failed miserably as I really couldn't bring myself to speak. I never imagined it could really be my Mom, but it was. Somehow my wife deciphered my bumbling and held me, tears in her eyes as well. I called my grandparents back and told them what happened. They were already packing to head up, but were going to leave in the morning because it was already afternoon. I told them I was heading out as soon as I got the car packed. They kept saying, "This is horrible," over and over again. I don't think they really knew what to do, none of us did. No parent should outlive their children, or their children's children. Even though this was their daughter-in-law, they were beside themselves. We all were…except for Katie.

We brought Katie and Abby into the living room and told them Nana had gone on to heaven. Abby was too young to understand what this meant, but Katie did, and her response was unexpected. She was smiling, while the rest of us had long faces on. She said, "I know, and it's okay, because she is with Jesus!"

There's something strangely comforting when a three-and-a-half-year-old tells you it's okay, that your Mom is with Jesus. I really can't explain it. Maybe something to do with the innocence and sincerity they speak with. Maybe because the night before she had heard directly from Jesus that my Mom was going to be with Him. Whatever it was, I can say I wasn't the only one who felt it, because throughout the funeral (which wound up delayed, due to a major ice storm that hit on the 7th and knocked out power to ninety-five percent of the county) Katie was a pillar of happiness and comfort, telling everyone who would listen that "It was okay. Nana is with Jesus." More importantly, she shared how she knew this personally because Jesus had told her before it happened. It was a difficult time made worlds better by my little angel, delivering a message of hope directly from God, offering a calming spirit for us all.

I spent the rest of my winter break with my Dad, helping him as best as I could. I can only imagine how hard it was for him, with the empty bed, the empty spot on the couch, the empty car seat and so many other areas of stark emptiness. I can only imagine how many times he turned around and called out for my Mom, expecting her to answer. They were planning to sell the house and travel, since the kids had grown up and now had families of their own. But now that would never happen.

Two months later, Katie came and told me that I had to call Poppa. When I asked her why, she replied, "Because God told me he's sad!" She went back to what she was doing, and I stood there looking oddly at her. She had a proven track record of hearing from God, but I thought, *Of course he's sad. He just lost the love of his life.*

From inside my spirit, however, I felt Katie's message was about something more. I walked quickly to the phone in the kitchen and dialed my father. When he got on the phone he was crying. My mother and father were high school sweethearts, married right after high school when began their new lives together. Thirty-two years later, they were still going strong. I wasn't really surprised he was crying. He cried at the funeral and later when I was up helping him around the house. I expected he would be crying for some time, I knew I would. But I could tell something was off about him, something was different. There was an…oddness…to his crying.

"What happened?" I asked.

He paused. "Rusty died."

I need to back up for a moment and explain who Rusty was and why he was important. To do that, I have to go back to a dog named Scruffy.

Scruffy was the large, white, curly-haired dog my parents had acquired from my brother several years prior. He'd gotten a free puppy and was responsible for feeding and walking him. Where my parents were living in the great outback of the north country of Peru, NY, walking meant just opening the door and letting the dog run. After my brother moved out to attend college and later live with his wife, the dog remained with my parents, having been fully assimilated into their family.

When Scruffy passed away my mom was completely heartbroken. My father was originally not sure what to do. Then someone suggested getting another dog. I do not remember where they got Rusty, but I do remember my mother picked him out and that he resembled the kinds of dog that she had always wanted. By the time that my mother crossed the rainbow bridge, they had Rusty for several years and he had bonded with both of my parents.

After my mother passed away, Rusty became my father's lifeline, someone to talk to and kind of be there for him. It may sound strange, but the dog really helped him through that first two months of losing his soulmate. In addition, I believe that Rusty represented the last connection that my father had to my mother since he had called Rusty her dog — and now he'd been hit by a car. I talked with my Dad for quite some time that day, doing my best to comfort him.

God is good, though, and about a month after this my Dad would visit a friend of his and wind up coming home with another dog. This friend knew he was lonely and needed a new dog after Scruffy had passed. Great friends do those kinds of things for you. They had offered him one earlier, but he kept refusing, so they kind of set him up.

As my father later recounted, he had gone to their home for dinner when his friend asked again if he wanted the dog. My dad again refused. It was at this point that the friend said okay, grabbed his shotgun and called Grizzly over. My Dad stopped him to ask what he was doing.

"We don't have the means to keep the dog," he said, "so I'm going to get rid of it!"

My Dad knew his friend had no intention of actually shooting the dog, but he agreed to take the dog nonetheless. Grizzly soon became his best friend, and continued to be for the next sixteen years. They were *inseparable*. I think after Grizzly passed, my Dad really lost his will to live, as it wasn't long after that he went to heaven.

This is a stone in my altar because Katie received two prophetic words from God, establishing her as the pillar of love, compassion, comfort and strength everyone needed during a really tough time. It helped show me the power of prophetic words, as well as the fact that the same God and power which can reside in me can also indwell and empower children who have accepted Him.

God didn't tell Katie my Mom was going to pass. Instead, He informed her that she was going to be safe and happy, living with him. These key phrases provided so much help to our hearts, and she only heard them because she was listening. I don't know if most of us in the family, as grown and mature adults, were too busy to hear God speaking. Or perhaps He simply wanted to use a little girl who was more than willing to help. Whatever the reason, Katie heard from God, and it helped my family cope with the loss. This event forged my faith, testifying that God would always be there for me, even if he had to use a child to speak to me.

ABBY FELL

'For I will restore you to health
And I will heal you of your wounds,' declares the Lord'
- Jeremiah 30:17a

Back when I was a senior in college, circa 1998-1999, Vicky would often take the girls to the park to let them play before picking me up from classes. The playground had some very unique equipment, one of which I called **The Inverted Monkey Bar Circle Ladder.** This ladder was a quarter circle arch that reached from the ground to a platform some 6+ feet off of the ground. On this ladder, about every two feet, was a half-circle, 1" thick metal ladder rung facing the ground. Honestly, this thing looked like a parent's nightmare, but my fearless girls would tackle it with the ease of Olympic gymnasts, and constantly use it as a means to get back up to the top so they could come down one of the slides. They *loved* this ladder and playground.

Until one fateful day.

On her return attempt, Abby didn't quite make it to the platform before losing her footing and falling...all six feet to the ground. My wife saw her fall, the scene playing out in slow motion. She first slipped forward, crashing down on the platform and slamming her collarbone before flipping backwards and finally landing on her back. Vicky immediately jumped up, grabbed both girls, packed them into the car and headed to pick me up. Again, this was well before cellphones were commonplace, so there was no calling ahead to tell me there was trouble.

As I approached the car, Vicky frantically explained what had happened. I went and checked Abby out. Now, I'm no doctor, but I did take first responder training and basic medical and field dressing class when I was young, many, many, *many* moons prior. I had at least a small working knowledge of the human anatomy, and did a quick assessment of Abby.

Her eyes were rolled back in her head. She wasn't lifting her head at all on her own, but letting it slump to one side. In addition, when I touched her chest her collarbone was…missing. To be sure I wasn't mistaken, I checked my own collarbone for the correct placement before rechecking Abby. When I touched Abby's upper chest again to feel for a collarbone, I found none, and she let out a small whimper. The only thing I could imagine was that she must have shattered her collarbone, because there wasn't anything of substance pushing. I hopped in the car and shifted into Mario Andretti mode, flooring the gas pedal as we raced to the nearest hospital.

As we pulled in, Vicky leapt out and grabbed Abby as I went to park the car with Katie. Before they left, I threw my arm behind me, placed my hand on Abby's head and simply said, "Jesus, heal her!" I honestly spoke that out way more in desperation than faith. I can be good in a crisis when it doesn't involve my family. When it does, I'm not the most faith-filled or rational person.

So when I prayed, it was out of sheer fear, because I knew her condition was serious. I parked the car in the first spot I could find, rapidly got Katie and headed into the ER. The waiting room was as far as I got, however because Katie was way too young to be allowed back in the emergency area. Again, no cell phones, so I didn't have any information on what was happening, nor could I really call anyone because I didn't have any change on me to use a payphone.

After what felt like an eternity, a nurse came out and said both Katie and I could go back to see Abby. This made me even more concerned, if they were allowing my little daughter back. My mind was racing the whole walk to the room. As I rounded the doorframe entering the room, I was immediately greeted by a doctor yelling at my wife. Why? Because, according to him, we'd just brought in a perfectly healthy child and were purposefully wasting not just his time, but the entire emergency staff's time and resources.

Well, watching someone yelling at my wife didn't sit well with me, especially since I knew there were issues with Abby. I immediately jumped in and told the doctor he was out of his mind and missed something. I reached over to my daughter's chest to show him how squishy the collarbone area was. I paused, in shock at what I felt.

Instead of mush, there was a collarbone. A firm, solid collarbone. The doctor exited the room while I continued to examine my daughter in utter disbelief. Granted, I probably should have noticed Abby was now sitting up and alert and playing with the doctor's stethoscope. It was at this moment, that this supposed man of faith, this Bible-believing, blood-bought saint, this Jesus-loving, spirit-filled man of God looked down at his daughter and realized He had healed her.

My mouth dropped. I wish I could tell you I expected it. (After all, I *did* pray.) Instead, I was preparing for the worse, mentally lining up who to call in our family and our church, planning on getting the pastor out to pray over my sick child. I was ready to see my daughter in pain, with months of casts and hospital stays and surgeries. Yet there I was, staring God's miracle right in the face, in utter and absolute shock.

We left the hospital shortly afterwards. Putting our kids in the car, I kissed my daughter and had to hold back the tears because I was so thankful to God. I praised God for healing my little girl.

This is a stone in my altar because it reminds me that God is a healing God. I didn't pray with power or earnest belief. I didn't pray down the heavens or command God move His mighty hands. Instead, I'd uttered a few words, not expecting anything from them, and yet

God responded. He might have responded even if I didn't pray, to be honest.

Either way, God responded and healed my girl. She wasn't in good shape when we arrived at the hospital, but left with happy, healthy smile on her face, and all because of God. Praise God!!

KATIE'S CHRISTMAS GIFT OF SNOW

'Then Jesus said to her, "O woman, your faith is great; it shall be done for you as you wish."'
- Matthew 15:28a

Thanksgiving 1999, I'd finished my bachelor's degree and was working full-time for a cellular company as an Electrical Engineer working on cell phones. Our church had helped us move from our original apartment into to a much larger, two-bedroom apartment in another complex, moving from Franklin Township to Edison. Everything seemed new to us because of the opportunities that were becoming available. When the holidays began to roll around, we couldn't have been more excited.

Christmas is our favorite time of the year. The movies, the decorations, the lights, everyone enjoying the season of love — we love it all! Sure, there are long lines and commercialism and egocentric greed, but I look past all that as we celebrate the birth of our savior — Jesus Christ.

One member of our family was especially excited. Just like she was every year, Katie was eagerly looking forward to Christmas and the fun time we would have as a family. Sure, there were presents, but to her it was about way more than that. We decided long before our kids were old enough to ask about Santa we would tell them the truth. We told them how it was Jesus's birthday, but He loved you so much that He wanted you to have presents on His special day. We also told them all about Santa Claus, and how he *was* fictional, but a tremendously fun fictional character at that.

Our kids never really waited to see Santa sneaking in at night because they knew the truth. We do wait until Christmas Eve after the kids go to bed to bring out and place the gifts, but they know full well they're from us. The primary reason we did this was because I hated being lied to as a kid. Hated it. On the day I found out the truth about the jolly fat man, I'd gotten in trouble for lying about something. That very night I heard a noise downstairs, so I sneaked out of my room and found my grandfather right there in the living room, bringing in all the toys.

When I questioned the present arrival the next day, my parents lied about it, insisting they were from Santa. I was fumingly upset, so much that I decided right then that I would vow to tell the truth to my own children. After becoming a Christian, it was just natural to tell our kiddos the truth. They never missed out on the Christmas joy, though, they just knew who was real and who wasn't. One benefit of this scenario was the ability to know what our kids wanted for Christmas ahead of time. Instead of writing a letter to Santa or whispering to one of his "helpers" at the mall, they would tell us directly. Today they provide us a list by the first of November of what they would like, and we're off shopping for presents.

Just before Thanksgiving, Katie, came to me and said what she really, *really* wanted for Christmas was snow. Not just a dusting or an inch of snow, mind you, but enough snow to make a snowman. We lived in central New Jersey at the time, and it was very possible to have a white Christmas. I told her the only one who could give her such a gift was God and Jesus, and she would need to pray to them to make it happen.

I didn't think at all about what might actually happen, or the fact that we hadn't seen a white Christmas in New Jersey for the previous ten years. I just told her that if she wanted it, to pray. This is what a

Spirit-filled, Jesus-loving Bible-believing, worship-song-singing, born-again father does ... right?

Well, Katie took this to heart and started praying every night before she went to bed. To be honest, I figured somewhere around the thirty day period from Thanksgiving to Christmas she would forget and *stop* praying about the snow, especially when she made her Christmas list for us.

She didn't.

She prayed *every night,* faithfully proclaiming to everyone that God was going to give her a white Christmas. The faith of a child. Man, we need more of that in the world these days.

About a week before Christmas, when Christmas Day was finally in the forecast, it wasn't looking good. During the day our temperatures were in the 50's, with it barely getting close to freezing at night. The forecast was bleak. As you probably know, for it to snow the air has to be freezing. For it to stick on the ground, however, the ground has to get super cold as well. Therefore, to get several inches of snow that would last required the temperature to start dropping to freezing and below. Ideally it would be dropping well below freezing at night, and hover around freezing throughout the day. However, our forecast had the lows in the mid to low 30', which meant we spent most, if not all of the day, above freezing. In short, the conditions were horrible for a snowstorm, and even worse for anything to stick to ground and actually accumulate. As you might imagine, I was watching the forecast like a hawk, saying some quiet prayers of my own.

As each day ticked by, nothing changed. This didn't affect Katie one bit, however, as she would just say the weatherman was wrong, adding, "Right, daddy?" I was like a deer in the headlights. What else could I reply, but, "That's right, Katie!" It was so adorably awesome that she was looking to me for approval, innocently unaware of the turmoil going on inside.

Looking at the reports, I grew increasingly worried. I was good to keep affirming her faith, as a father would and should do, but mine was stuck on the hard science of the weather forecast, and no matter how one looked at it wasn't going to come anywhere close to snow weather. Secretly I began trying to figure out how I would let her down when the snow didn't arrive. I'd settled on saying something along the lines of, "Sometimes, for the sake of everyone else, God has to say no to us." I wasn't even convincing myself, but it was the best I could come up with.

Christmas Eve arrived like a freight train, busted brakes and barreling down a track with the bridge out up ahead. I hadn't come up with any better response to the situation, and the forecast hadn't changed. I had hoped the seven or five or even three day forecast would change. But on the day before, it was rare to see a change in what the weather men were predicting.

I'd been practicing my excuse for why it hadn't snowed as we entered the church building for the Christmas Eve evening service, the temperature outside a balmy 50 degrees with clear skies. I remember looking around at the bare-naked trees and cold, stained grass, wondering at what point I was going to break it to Katie that her snow wasn't coming after all.

Worship was great, but I was too focused on how I was going to break my daughter's heart that I really didn't get into it. In fact, I barely knew where we were in the service, due to being so hyperfocused on Katie.

Suddenly the pastor took the pulpit, stopping the musicians as they prepped for another classic Christmas song. I looked up, thinking maybe he had a word from the Lord or perhaps he was going to read some of the Christmas story from the Bible, but I was wrong. Instead, waving his hands to stop, he declared, "We have to stop!"

He took a breath, placing his hands down on the pulpit and announced, "I'm terribly sorry, but we're going to have to send everyone home and cancel the remainder of the service. It is *snowing* outside, and it doesn't look to be letting up!"

Wait!? *What?!*

Did the pastor just say it was snowing outside? For that to be the case, it would mean that the air temperature had to drop some twenty degrees! On top of that, storm clouds had to have rolled in in record time, because the sky had been super clear when we entered the church. If that wasn't enough, for it to be bad enough to stop church, the ground temperature had to drop significantly as well, in order for the snow to stick and become potentially hazardous.

To top all of that off, it had to all happen in less than thirty minutes we had been in service. It all seemed impossible. It's not that the weather can't change rapidly, because it can and does. Storm clouds could come out of nowhere. Temperatures could drop.

But for all of those to happen *at once*, concurrently — especially the ground freezing over — well, in all my life that's the only time I've *ever* seen all of them happen simultaneously. I knew it was God!

The pastor continued apologizing, "For everyone's safety, we just can't keep you here any longer. Please drive safe and have a very merry WHITE CHRISTMAS!!" With those last words, he headed down off of the altar to his family.

I gathered my family and rushed out of the sanctuary and down the front entrance steps. I couldn't believe my eyes. *It was snowing.* It was snowing, and it wasn't just lightly dusting the ground, the snow was really coming down, so strong it was almost difficult to see the cars. There was already a white layer covering most everything and the roads were looking increasingly unsafe. It was surreal, and I was in shock as I ushered my family toward our car to head home.

Personally, I love living in Texas where it's warm to hot most of the year. However, I think the world looks most gorgeous when it's been snowing for a while and everything is covered in a fresh blanket of white. Especially when everyone has gotten home and it's still light outside. The snow is falling. It's silent and serene. Peaceful. Beautiful. I've seen some great things on this planet, but for by far that's the prettiest.

We left the church along with everyone else and made our way home as quick as we possibly could with the snow and roads being slick. As we walked into the apartment, we quickly turned on the news. Every weather man said the same thing, "A freak storm came out of nowhere and was blanketing the area with snow." Channel by channel, weather person by weather person, all exclaiming the same shock.

I was honestly in disbelief at what my eyes were seeing. By morning we had almost a foot of snow covering the entire area. I was beside myself. I knew I told my daughter to pray, and I knew that God was able to make it snow. I just didn't believe it would happen. I didn't have the faith to believe. Katie, on the other hand, did. And now she was smiling from ear to ear at the storm that had dropped her Christmas present.

Ever since the moment the announcement at church came, Katie had been telling people as we left that the snow was God's present to her. Church people were courteous to Katie, but would then give me a look I knew all too well. You know, the one that asks, "What are you teaching that poor child?"

Well, apparently, I was teaching her that her dad needs a lesson on faith, because God was answering her prayers as she believed without wavering once that He was going to send snow. When we got home, Katie wasn't anything but smiles the entire time. The next morning — Christmas Morning — she proudly proclaimed, "God gave me snow for His birthday!"

Yes, oh yes, He did.

This is a stone in my altar because, while God was answering Katie's prayer, He was teaching me a huge lesson on faith. Katie simply did what the Bible says to do.

'Truly I say to you, whoever says to this mountain, 'Be taken up and cast into the sea,' and does not doubt in his heart, but believes that what he says is going to happen, it will be granted him. Therefore I say to you, all things for which you pray and ask, believe that you have received them, and they will be granted you. '

- Mark 11:23-24

She believed even when I didn't, and God gave her what she had asked for in prayer. The irony of this for me was that by "acting" like a spirit-believing and led father, telling Katie to pray actually caused *me* to become a much better spirit-believing and led father full of faith. Praise God.

UNLISTED LISTED NUMBER

'Be anxious for nothing, but in everything by prayer and supplication with thanksgiving let your requests be made known to God. '
- Philippians 4:6

June 2000, we were living in a rental house, provided by the elderly couple from church we were attending. They had an unlisted phone in their name that we were allowed to use. I didn't give it out, but used it to call on jobs. (Well, mostly technical recruiters, because most companies went through them). My idea was the recruiter would be able to weed out and select the good candidates to present to the companies. I must have spoken with upwards around four dozen recruiters. Not even kidding. But none of them provided me any job leads or interviews with companies.

So, the house was a very old and small, with two bedrooms upstairs and a living room and kitchen downstairs. The stairs leading to the second floor were extremely narrow, to the point where it almost felt like you were going up a ladder. Walking up and down them was a constant challenge. Still, we were thankful to have a roof over our heads, even if it was a temporary one.

One day the phone rang. I'd momentarily toyed with not answering it, as I could count on one hand the number of people who had the number and would be calling for me. After some debate, I answered it and to my surprise it was a very close friend of mine who I hadn't seen or heard from since we moved to New Jersey to attend Rutgers. I was excited to hear his voice, as this period in our lives was difficult and he brought back many fond memories of staying up all night role playing. He was the kind of friend that would give you the shirt off his back if you asked him to or he saw the need. When we left for New Jersey, his wife had been accepted into the Navy, and he was off to Louisiana (I believe). Receiving a call from him alone lifted my spirits.

I was confused how he reached me, however, as the phone was unlisted. "How did you get this number?" I asked. He replied he looked me up on the internet. Now to understand, you have to think back to 2000 (if you were alive back then) and what the "internet" looked like. Google was in its infancy, and to have looked me up sounded almost implausible by itself, let alone the fact that the phone wasn't in my name. This doesn't even take in to account the fact that there were a fraction of a percent of the sites back then, when compared to the ones that exist today.

However, somehow — ahem, *God* — my friend found my number and called me. I must have sounded crazy, because I think I asked him like a dozen times how he got the number. He patiently answered the same thing, every time.

He was calling to tell me about all the amazing employment opportunities he'd discovered in the Dallas-Fort Worth (DFW) Texas area. He and his wife had just recently moved there, as it was being called the Silicon Valley of the Mid-West. He knew I went to school for Electrical Engineering and that there were no shortage of tech companies and jobs. In fact, at the time there was a shortage of technical people, which made it a job seekers market.

It was exciting to hear about all the opportunities my friend shared with me. In addition, he said I could crash on his couch any time as I searched for a job. (Great friends do these kinds of things.) I got his number and hung up the phone with mixed feelings.

On the one hand, there was a huge part of me that wanted to jump on this opportunity because something about it seemed right, not to mention I know my friend wouldn't be exaggerating. On the other hand, we wanted to be near family, because it's extremely helpful in life to be near family. Moving from New York to Texas would effectively cut us off from our roots. Sure, we could always visit, but plane tickets weren't cheap.

Vicky had been downstairs when I took the call, and afterwards I immediately sought her out. I explained how our friend was basically telling us to load up the family and move to Texas. I knew Vicky enjoyed being near her family, and I wouldn't want to break that up if she wasn't on board with the idea. After some discussion and a tiny bit of prayer, she said, "Well, open up your resume and let's see what God does!" "Opening up" meant updating it to indicate I was willing to relocate, thus "opening" my resume up to any company in the country.

I was honestly not prepared for what happened next.

I'd spend four and a half months looking in every corner of upstate New York for a job, and only received one interview (and even that didn't end well). I added my phone number to my resume and hoped for the best. Over the next twenty-four hours, I received **over 40 calls** from companies who wanted to interview me. Somewhere around ninety percent of them were from the DFW area. Vicky and I felt like this was God putting a gigantic arrow before us to follow. We began to look into how we would get to Texas and go to some of these interviews.

This is a stone in my altar to remind me that no matter where you go, God can always send help. I can't think of any way outside of God's divine intervention that my friend would have ever found the number to where we were staying. But God made sure that he found us so that He could send us directions and help. Honestly, it was like something out of a movie.

The star is down on his luck and things look bleak, and then all of a sudden a ray of hope shows up (usually in the form of a person who could have been a former friend, co-worker, classmate, etc.) and offers him a lifeline. My friend called at one of the most desperate times of my life, extending a lifeline that radically changed my family's lives for the better. It was such a God thing!

ENTERTAINING ANGELS

'Let love of the brethren continue. Do not neglect to show hospitality to strangers,
for by this some have entertained angels without knowing it.'
- Hebrews 13:1-2

We had no money and really no place to stay, but needed to somehow get to Texas, camp out on my friend's couch, and score some interviews. Now, if I'd waited long enough, there was a good chance some company would fly me out for an onsite interview, but time was of the essence, as my family didn't have any income.

We needed a plan. And we needed help.

A lot of help.

After praying, we knew this help would need to come from family, because we'd left all of our friends at the time and my Texas friend wasn't yet in a position where he could help us out, financially.

When we thought and prayed about it, there was really only one person who potentially had the money to help us get to Texas and back, and that was my grandfather. That's not to say we couldn't have enlisted everyone in the family to give us *something* and possibly have raised enough money to make the trip. However, my grandfather was a candidate who most likely just had it all on hand. There was, however, a problem: he didn't approve of us moving away from New Jersey.

He didn't want to be twenty-four hours away from his great grandkids, instead of only an hour and a half. We didn't know this at the time, but he was also beginning to have trouble seeing, and had already been involved in some minor accidents. The longer drive pretty much meant he wouldn't see his great grandkids. Texas was a lot farther than just up the New York Thruway to outside of Albany.

Vicky and I arrived at my grandfather's house by ourselves. We didn't want to have this discussion with the kids running around, causing any distractions. Plus, there was nowhere for the kids to stay if we brought them. So we left them with Vicky's older brother and made the trip. I remember sitting on the couch asking his assistance in driving to Texas and interview, see how the employment climate was and come back. We had estimated the gas, hotel, food and anything else we could think of.

We had a plan.

All we needed were the finances.

At first he wasn't interested in helping us. However, by the end of the visit he'd completely changed his mind and handed us the money. He made it clear this was the last of the money he could give us, and if we got in a financial pickle in the future, there was no more. We acknowledged this, thanking them for the money and drove home.

On Monday, July 3rd, 2000, Vicky and I were on the road to Texas! My mother-in-law had helped us get our first cellular phone so we could not only receive calls from prospective employers, but also call for help if we needed it. As we drove, I received a few calls for interviews — all but one was for the Dallas-Fort Worth (DFW) area, further confirming for us God was directing us there.

We had a giant book of maps in our hands and a planned the route to take. Our plan had us traveling down the Appalachian trail along Interstate 81 until we hit the great state of Tennessee. We would then hang a right onto Interstate 40 and continue our trek west. After Memphis and halfway through Arkansas, we would then turn off onto

Interstate 30 and ride it all the way into Texas and meet up with my friend and his wife. It was all pretty straightforward, only... there was a major hiccup along the way.

A few miles down the I-40 heading west, after spending the night in Nashville, the car suddenly started overheating. I don't remember for sure, but I think there was an alert, a light and the gage that indicated we were running way too hot. Not being a car guy but having learned a thing or two about dashboards, I knew this was bad. If left unchecked, the car would fully overheat and shut down with steam and stuff coming out of the engine.

God allowed me to remember a few things that my Dad had told me. First, turn on the heat in the car, because the heater would then siphon heat off of the engine. Second, roll down the windows because it was about to get infinitely hotter in the car. And finally, pop the hood but *do not open it entirely*, leaving the latching lever in place to prevent it from flying upward. This way you can circulate more air flow over the engine, effectively cooling it down.

So we did all these things and continued rolling down the Tennessee highway, the temperature outside a balmy 90 plus degrees. This didn't change the fact that we had a major issue which needed to get fixed *fast*, or else we would wind up having a much larger issue, potentially one which would cost a ton of money and strand us with no way to get to Texas *or* home.

We began looking for a service station at one of the exits. Exit after exit, we saw nothing. Plenty of gas stations, restaurants and places to lay our heads, but not a single service stations for miles and miles. We were praying hard.

Finally, we saw a building at an exit, huge words written across the roof, "Service Here!" This was going to be the answer to our prayers! We immediately exited the highway, pulled up and I raced out of the car. I entered the establishment, only to quickly discover... they didn't service cars.

They were a big rig service center to help stranded truckers. I must have looked visibly deflated, as the clerk was quick to inform me he knew of a good reputable place just a few miles from where we were. Without even waiting for me to acknowledge, he began to give me directions.

"Head down this road here for about a half mile and make a left at the corner store. Continue down that road and just as you leave the pavement..."

"Wait, what?! Leave the pavement?" I asked. This was an alien concept for an urbanite like myself. But the directions didn't end there.

"As you leave the pavement," the clerk continued, "you will see a giant tree. You'll want to keep going for about two miles, then when you come upon a second huge tree, immediately past there on your right will be the garage."

I must have looked stunned, because he repeated the directions and then added, "Trust me you can't miss this place!" As I walked out of there every horror movie I should never have watched was racing through my mind. The only conclusion I could come to was no one would ever hear from us again. Still, despite a part of me screaming internally in terror, there was something else inside screaming it would be alright. To be honest, I had no other options. So I got in the car and headed down the road.

Ten minutes later, I was pulling up to this little shack of a place that had an alarming number of abandoned cars in its backyard. If it wasn't for the tiny little garage door, I would have been certain we hadn't found the correct place. Every detail the clerk laid out had played out in front of us, one after the other, until we pulled in front of the small home next to the huge tree.

The unfolding horror movie in my head said we should turn away and run, but before fear or anxiety could get a grip of my soul, the nicest elderly lady came out to greet us. It was as if she had been expecting us. I assumed at the time the clerk called ahead, but today I just think this was all part of God's plan and they were all somehow in the know. I explained the car was overheating and we needed to get it repaired.

"Pa!" she hollered out, tilting her head slightly towards the back of the building. A few moments later, a slender, medium height man in overalls appeared from the back. "Car in the drive is overheating!" she said.

With that, the man took our keys and disappeared. With nothing else to do but wait, my wife and I sat down in the small customer area in the front of the building. I remember being surprised by the fact that every inch of the wall in front of us was covered with car pictures and posters. Even the vintage-looking soda pop machine had car pictures on it. I can still see that little waiting room when I close my eyes, it was so unique.

I think it's important to describe this waiting room's feeling. When I was outside, I was nervous and anxious and afraid of how much this was going cost, money we didn't budget for repairs. When I was inside, however, the warmest, calmest, sweetest sensation washed over me. It's hard to explain, but sitting in that car-covered room, I felt like everything was going to work out and everything was right with the world.

It was the best experience that I'd ever had, and words truly do not do it justice. Even though there were a lot of thoughts going through our minds about money and what was going to happen, they no longer felt like they were an issue, or even pressing. Outside, the weight of the world was on top of us and it was hard to breath. However, inside it was like the outside didn't matter. A nuclear blast could wipe out the world outside and it would be alright, because it was so peaceful and serene inside.

I shot a glance at Vicky, and I could see in her eyes that her mind was going a million miles a minute. I'd thought it was because we were, beyond a doubt, in the most amazing, good-feeling-filled, nicest little place in the creepiest location we'd ever been in.

I put my hand on hers to hopefully provide her with some reassurance everything would work out. It didn't help.

The elderly lady must have also felt my wife's tension, as she soon struck up a conversation. "You're not from around here, are you?"

It was as if Niagara Falls had been damned up for months and suddenly set free. My wife began telling this nice lady our life story in extreme detail, all the way up to how we had arrived at their doorstep.

The lady listened with great intent, as if she was hearing the single greatest story outside of Jesus that had ever been spoken.

As my wife finished, she came over to me and pulled me close. "You realize," she whispered, "that depending on the amount of the repairs, we may not have enough to pay!"

No. No, I hadn't realized that.

Or maybe I hadn't acknowledged the possibility because I knew car repairs were costly. I was too busy soaking up the calm. However, this was coupled with the fact that we had made a serious miscalculation when we determined how much to borrow from my grandfather. We had assumed prices in the New York and New Jersey area would be a good indicator of how much it would be the entire route down to Texas.

We were wrong.

As we sat there, we knew there was only a few hundred dollars left in the account and time was ticking against us. Vicky had worked at a towing and service company as a receptionist and bookkeeper, so she knew they charged not just for parts but also by the hour. While they are totally worth the money, it was more a matter of us lacking funds that caused our concern. My wife grabbed the single cell phone and walked outside to call her family and have them on standby, just in case we needed their help.

After several hours, the repairs were finally completed. When you're watching the hours tick by, slapping you hard with each one passing, time slows to a crawl, slowly tightening a grip around your throat. But the wait was over and the car was done. All that remained before blowing out of the place and getting back on the road was to pay the bill. Both my wife and I cringed as the nice lady began to ring up it up. She stopped typing far sooner than either of us expected.

"That will be $82 even!"

"Are you sure?" Vicky inquired, shooting me a very puzzling look.

"Quite sure!" The lady smiled as she tilted her head, staring at Vicky for what felt like an eternity. I wanted to jump in and ask what was going on, but I didn't. Mostly because I wasn't really even sure what to ask.

"Okay," my wife relented, digging out the card to pay. Later I asked my wife why she questioned the bill, and had been so tensely staring the old lady down. She informed me that when she looked over the invoice of the repairs, she immediately recognized this garage used the exact same coding scheme the place she worked at used. This couple was only charging us for the cost of the thermostat.

No markup on the part. No labor costs. Just the wholesale pricing on the part itself, and she was shocked. In addition, the man worked on our car for a lot longer than it takes to replace a thermostat. Vicky had been convinced we were going to get a huge bill full of parts and labor, raking us over the proverbial coals. That wasn't the case. I can tell you this, he serviced much more than the thermostat. Our car never ran better during the entire time we had owned it.

Moments later we were getting into the car as the couple said their goodbyes, telling us not to worry and everything was going to be just fine. I have to tell you, I let out a huge sigh of relief when we got back on pavement. I mean, I guess a road is a road and the people were very nice and the waiting room was supernaturally peaceful, but it felt very odd leaving the pavement to this city boy. Thankfully, it was all done and we were on our way.

As we approached the interstate, Vicky turned to me. "We have a problem!"

"Not another one!"

She had done the math on how much everything had cost up to this point in gas, lodging and food, coupled with how far we had to go and determined we were going to be short. She explained we had enough money to get to Texas or enough to go back home, but not both.

We paused, sitting there at the stop sign just before the on ramp to the interstate, looking at each other in shock and dismay. Then we clasped hands and prayed. We agreed God called us to go, and wanted to continue the journey, despite what it looked like. After all, a couple of kind strangers had just told us everything was going to be just fine. As I turned the car and sped up the onramp, Vicky said, "We are Texas or bust!"

Fortunately, God had better plans for us.

Today Vicky and I firmly believe we entertained angels when we went to that little service station off the beaten path. We really can't fully explain why, but when we were in their presence there was this amazing peace that everything was right where it was supposed to be and everything would work out just fine. Couple that with the way the car was repaired beyond just the thermostat and the price, and it all added up to being Godly.

But even if we're incorrect and they were just a very nice elderly couple, there was plenty of other things that demonstrated how God and his angels were with us. First was how far we drove without a working thermostat. Second, the encounter with the clerk when he told me to trust him lit up my spirit and convinced me I should believe him.

Third, the couple who was so nice and fixed our car and having the exact part we needed on hand. Fourth, while we were overall short for a return trip, the amount we were charged was a God send. Finally, that we completed our trip and arrived in Texas. All of those things add up to God watching over us and sending his angels to surround and protect and guide us.

This is a huge stone in my altar because it reminds me that even in the toughest situations, God sends help. We are never in this alone, and if we listen and pray and follow, God will always see us through. It may not be the way we expected, or it might be in the presence of angels. Regardless, God will never leave you or forsake you. Thank you Lord.

HERE COMES BLESSING NUMBER 3

'But the angel said to him, "Do not be afraid, Zacharias,
for your petition has been heard, and your wife Elizabeth will bear you a son, and
you will give him the name John. You will have joy and gladness, and many will
rejoice at his birth. '
- Luke 1:13-14

In November 2001, I was laid off from my job, alongside approximately forty thousand others from the Cellular company. While I'd prayed and hoped to remain with the company, it wasn't meant to be. They were super good with a severance package, however, extending our health insurance for another six months. Suddenly finding myself with an ample amount of free time on my hands, I figured I would take the holidays to enjoy the family, then find a job right after the first of the year. Again, it was a boom time for skilled computer people and I had the benefit of being able to work both the hardware or software sides. Little did I know what was about to happen.

October 2001, and the Enron scandal broke. I'm not going to claim to understand what all was involved, but shortly afterwards Arthur Anderson, Enron's accounting firm, was implicated. Over the next several months lawsuits would fly and handfuls of companies would go under. Around this time the telecom bubble burst, taking with it an influx of jobs all centered around the newly emerging internet, suddenly flooding the market with out of work engineers and developers.

By January 2002, a market which earlier had two jobs for every worker now had around a hundred plus workers *for every job*. Obviously if I known this was coming, I would have tried to find a job immediately after being laid off. However, even through all of this chaos, God was good to us.

In April 29th, 2002, all of the severance and insurance had run out. I was on unemployment and thankful for it, but it was severely lacking compared to our needs. We were struggling as now a family of four as God has blessed us with two daughters who were now eight and six years old. We were visiting food shelves, using any and all services we could get, which was only WIC because everything else we disqualified for, due to how much I made on unemployment. It most definitely was *not* a good time to become pregnant. (Insert foreshadowing music here...)

This is when we visited a woman's health clinic because Vicky appeared to be in the early stages of menopause. The nurse practitioners confirmed we were done having children, as Vicky's system was effectively shutting down. We were super blessed to have any children at all, let alone two amazing girls. After checking out my wife and doing tests to prove she wasn't pregnant, they prescribed the drug Depo Provera. The reason they had to be sure that Vicky wasn't pregnant was because this drug would essentially force the body to abort a baby if she were carrying one.

So we knew for sure that at the end of April, Vicky was *not* pregnant. She took the Provera for the first ten days as prescribed, and very shortly after that she began to feel really sick. She was afraid she might have a stomach bug. Because of this (and an inner feeling, God possibly speaking to her spirit), she decided not to return to the clinic or take any more of the Provera.

June 1st, 2002, and Vicky was having all day sickness — the kind she'd only experienced when she was pregnant. She was convinced it was a stomach bug, however, I felt strongly that she was pregnant. I informed her of this, and she quickly dismissed it because the clinic had confirmed she was in the early stages of menopause. She reasoned what she was feeling was very possibly due to that, adding there is no way she could be pregnant because we had just gotten rid of all of Katie and Abby's baby stuff. Nonetheless, I couldn't shake the feeling. So I offered what felt like a compromise: I would go to the store and get a pregnancy test to at least rule out pregnancy as the cause.

She agreed after some convincing, because at that point any extra expense was highly scrutinized. While in the store staring at the different tests, God spoke to me and said, "Get two!"

Get two?! Why would I need two?

Vicky had never had a false positive. One should be plenty. But God insisted that we needed two of them. So I grabbed the only double pack on the shelf — thankfully on sale — and began wondering if perhaps we had a friend who might need the second test later. I surmised there must be a reason for it, after all.

Arriving home, I handed Vicky the dual pack and she was confused. Being quick on my feet, I told her a half-truth, and explained that it was on sale (which was true) and cheaper this way. Normally, my wife and I would counsel couples to never lie or present half-truths (because half-truths are half lies), however, given that it was hard enough to convince her to buy one to begin with, I felt this was the best course of action for following what God told me.

She grabbed the box with the combined force of Wonder Woman and Supergirl, as if striking down a villain. For me, her sudden outburst of emotion only confirmed that she was, in fact, quite pregnant.

Time passed. More time passed. And then some *more* time passed, and I began to think that maybe I should go and check on her when she suddenly emerged from the bathroom, an inexplicable look of dread look on her face.

"I'm pregnant!"

At these words I began to cheer… while she started to cry. And they were not happy tears.

Remember, I was out of job and my wife's job had just ended. We had no insurance. We had no way to pay for a doctor, should we have even been able get an appointment (doctor's offices tend to not schedule you when you have no insurance). To make this worse, all of Vicky's pregnancies, including the ones we lost, were all high risk. We had already lost two children due to miscarriages. In truth, we were in a very bad spot, both from a medical and worldly perspective. Fortunately, God was on our side and He had a completely different perspective.

I suggested to Vicky that she could take the second one in the morning and see if the results were the same. She scowled at me. "I already took them both, because I didn't believe the first one!"

I suddenly understood why God wanted me to get *two* tests. This meant that WE WERE PREGNANT — again — even after the doctors told us it was impossible. *Again.*

God obviously had a different plan, and we honestly weren't sure how to feel. This was one of those moments where everything inside you is telling you to trust God, while every single piece of evidence and your flesh is screaming that you're in deep boiling water with no way out. By all logical conclusions, you're going to die, a slow and terrible death.

Try as one may, it's incredibly hard to silence the mind when you're faced with these types of situations. But we strive hard to keep focused on God and help each other keep our focus on God. Not an easy task, but a worthwhile one. The good news is that God wouldn't leave us hanging.

On Tuesday, June 4th, we arrived back at the clinic where they had told us Vicky was going through menopause, only this time for an appointment about our newly found pregnancy. They were super excited for us, and informed us we needed an OBGYN doctor. Knowing our situation, they instructed us to go to social services to request medical coverage for the pregnancy.

On Wednesday, June 5th, after spending an entire day at the Department of Human Services, we were told my unemployment check was about twenty dollars over their limit, so they wouldn't be providing us any help. We were shocked. We had lived on welfare before, even while I was working at a minimum wage job when we had the girls. To be told that there was no help for us with our current pregnancy amidst all the difficulties was earth-shattering.

The worldly voices were hard to overcome at this point, even though God kept informing us that He was with us. Human Services directed us to the JPS network, who helped people without insurance. We began to feel like there was a glimmer of hope... until we called them. We explained our situation, and the first available appointment they could get for us was October.

OCTOBER?!?! It was *June*! Knowing her history, there was an extremely good chance Vicky would have lost the baby by October. We told them that wasn't good enough, and they promptly hung up the phone.

We hit the floor on our knees in prayer. God had a plan, we just didn't know what it was.

Thursday June 6th, I opened a phone book (yes, an actual paper phone book) and grabbed the phone. I called every doctor in the yellow pages (yellow pages were for businesses, while white pages were for people) looking for *any* doctor who would take my wife. Once hearing the answer to a few questions which usually included "Do you have insurance?" and "Do you have any known medical issues?" or "Have any previous pregnancies had complications?", they would quickly turn us down for an appointment.

Out of all the women's doctors in the phone book (a good three dozen), only one would agree to see us because Vicky happened to have been to that office a year prior. They did have conditions, however. The doctor (or the office) wanted five hundred dollars up front, plus an additional five hundred for each visit and we were to cover the cost of any tests or anything they did.

I informed the receptionist we didn't have that kind of money, to which they coldly told us those were the conditions. This left us without medical options whatsoever, except for showing up in the emergency room when Vicky went into labor (assuming we lasted that long). To say we were praying a lot was an understatement.

We felt overwhelmed and out of options. We had only moved to the area two years prior, and still didn't know very many people nor had a good church family yet. God never left our side constantly opening doors and clearing obstacles for us. While this gave us a tremendous sense that we were going to somehow make it, we still felt the lack of a solid support structure around us making things exponentially more stressful.

We discovered my wife has a hormone deficiency that caused her body to see the baby as a foreign invading entity, instead of an actual growing human who's supposed to be there. Because of this, she needed to be on special hormones supplements when pregnant — hormones which could only be obtained with a prescription from the doctor.

We prayed, and God directed us to a man I knew who happened to be a holistic healer. I'd done some computer work for him, but hadn't considered him at first because I didn't think he had access to the hormone, nor could he get them in the quantities that Vicky needed. However, God kept urging me to reach out to him, after which he gladly took Vicky as a patient.

He did an assessment of her condition and gave us a bunch of creams and drops, with instructions she was to apply them several times a day to places all over her body (the back of her knees and elbows, under her tongue, etc.) Honestly, we weren't even sure they would work, but God is amazing. They not only worked for immediate relief, but helped keep Vicky's body in check *throughout* the pregnancy. In addition, this doctor charged us using the barter system, so I contributed my computer and graphic skills for his medical skills as he helped Vicky. This was an absolute blessing.

As the pregnancy progressed, we became in need of greater care for Vicky and the baby. This is when God brought a certified midwife into our lives. She was a member of one of the churches we had attended for a period of time. She hadn't originally heard we were pregnant, and we didn't think of her initially because we barely knew her. As soon as she found out, she immediately reached out and began caring for Vicky, *free of charge.*

She was a godsend, being able to do things like letting us hear the heartbeat, providing prenatal vitamins, and a host of other services associated with being pregnant that we typically didn't have access too. I was so thankful we were surrounded by so many professionals, walking through this with our third birth. If this had been our first pregnancy, I would have lost it early on. No question, I'd have been committed to the crazy house, the one with all those fancy pillow walls.

The midwife later pointed us to a sonogram school that was looking for patients willing to have a group of students watch as the images were taken, giving them some real clinical experience. Again, this was also absolutely free. So in the middle of having no money, no insurance and no job, God provided a free-of-charge sonogram of the baby.

After all we were walking through, I can't express how amazing it was to see his little feet and hands on that screen. I'd seen these images with my previous two kids, but there was something different this time around. I think it was because this time we were in such a whirlwind of miracles, constantly in our face.

Both of our girls had just as many miracles, of course, but we weren't in such financial dire straits, as we had both a doctor and state insurance. During the exam they asked if we wanted to know if it was a boy or girl, and being traditionalists we said didn't want to know. However, during the exam the sonographer accidentally announced, "Whoop there it is!" She tried to play it off, embarrassed at the gaff, but we kind of knew at that point we were likely having a boy.

On Monday September 9th, I started a new job as a software developer for Helicopter manufacturer. I would be working on the flight control software as part of a team responsible for components in the two military grade vertical lift aircraft. It was a real cool job because I've always loved helicopters (ever since my dad and I used to watch Airwolf and movies like Blue Thunder). In addition, this job came with the added bonus of my insurance coming into effect the very first day of employment. What's more, it didn't have any pre-existing conditional clauses, meaning the pregnancy from that moment on would be covered. *WOW!* Praise God!

Vicky returned to calling doctors, but surprisingly got the same run around — even *with* insurance. We figured this was due to being four months pregnant and having had complications in the past.

However, the one doctor who she had seen in the past finally made an appointment with us because we were already patients.

On our first visit, they did a complete workup and everything checked out to be good. The only thing we differed on was the due date. We knew weren't pregnant on April 29th, but were definitely pregnant on June 1st, meaning it was sometime in May that we conceived. This meant the due date was likely sometime in February, but based on the sonogram, the doctor said we were due in late December. Our midwife later explained that Vicky's gestational diabetes could cause the measurements to falsely read farther along. The doctor knew this, but for whatever reason didn't acknowledge it. It didn't matter to us, however, because we had a doctor to cover us for the rest of the pregnancy, so we were thrilled either way.

On October 31st — yes, on Halloween — we were at Walmart shopping. While I was watching the girls, Vicky had gone to the restroom. On her way, she slipped and fell on some soapy liquid on the floor (and especially hard to see for a pregnant woman). Once down, she was unable to get up, even with the help of the store staff. The manager had me paged, and I immediately came to the front of the store.

Vicky felt terrible, and was even having light contractions. We immediately went home and called the doctor's office, who told us if she wasn't bleeding we should be fine, but to keep monitoring how Vicky was feeling. Climbing into bed that night, we noticed she had what looked like bruising on her legs and was extremely sore. We prayed about it and went to sleep.

First thing in the morning we checked on her condition to find all signs of bruising were gone, as well as the soreness that she'd been feeling. In addition, the contractions had stopped and there was no blood. God had protected the baby and healed my wife.

A few weeks later Vicky called me at work.

"Hi honey," I began after discovering who was on the phone.

"You're not gonna believe what just happened," Vicky replied.

"What?"

"I locked the keys in the trunk of the car."

"Well, just use my keys." I knew she had them on her because of other events in the day.

"I can't...because your keys are locked in the trunk!"

"Okay, then just use your keys, honey," I added, feeling like I was solving the problem of the day.

"I can't do that either...because they're also in the trunk."

"Okay, let me get this straight," I said, trying really hard not to laugh. "Both sets of keys are now locked in the trunk?"

"Yes."

It was a terrible situation, but we both broke out laughing.

Fortunately God reminded me I had a spare key in my wallet. A potentially stressful event, but that moment of laughter in the middle of our constant chaos was a total blessing!

It was December 14th, and we were still arguing with the doctor over the due date. We knew it had to be sometime in early February, whereas the doctor was insistent it was December 26th. This would become extremely important. If the baby did, in fact, arrive in December the child would be a premature baby, but not *classified* as one, and therefore would not qualify to receive the treatment the baby might need.

So when my wife came out of the bedroom, having changed her clothes for the second time because she was supposedly "sweating" in December, (a very real possibility in Texas), I knew her water had broken and we needed to go to the hospital. I would later learn that she knew this also, but also knew once she got to the hospital they wouldn't be giving her food and wanted to have an early dinner before leaving. While she was employing this subterfuge, she had me actually call the doctor's office to find out if they had a test to differentiate between amniotic fluid and sweat. As it turns out, they did...but you needed to go to the hospital for them to test. Finally, after she ate what she wanted as her "last meal," she agreed to go to the hospital, dropping the girls off at friends. It was time! We were on our way!

Sure enough, Vicky's water broke and the baby would be arriving in the next twenty-four hours. Here's an interesting note on how God works for our good. Our beloved doctor — "Doctor D" —delivered both Katie and Abby in upstate New York. During her pregnancy, Vicky often told God that she really wished "Doctor D" could deliver the baby. We arrived at the hospital to find our doctor was on vacation, and the doctor who was subbing for her had a last name beginning with a D. So it turned out our baby was *also* delivered by "Doctor D." A different doctor, sure, but it was still a neat answer to prayer, and this substitute doctor was equally amazing.

Shortly after arriving, Vicky was hooked up, an internal monitor was placed on the baby, and an epidural was on the way. Everything was set. Well...almost everything. Her water broke, but the baby wasn't fully in position, which translated to a long night ahead of us as Vicky's body worked to put the child in position. It's really amazing how God designed a woman's body to do all this stuff when creating and birthing a baby. It was an absolute miracle to watch each of my children being born.

On December 15th in the early afternoon, things were coming down to the wire. It had been almost twenty-four hours since Vicky's water broke, and if we couldn't birth the baby natural they would have to perform an emergency C-Section, which no one in the room or hospital wanted to happen. At almost the last moment, the baby was finally in position, and we could finally push. Only...there was a problem. When Vicky pushed, the baby's heartbeat dropped to almost nothing.

Judging from all the professionals in the room, this was *not* a good thing. So they would have Vicky rest for a few moments in between pushes, in hopes of giving the baby's heart enough time to recover. This worked, but it was still trending lower and taking longer for the baby to recover each time. Finally the doctor stated, "One more push, and if the child doesn't come out we'll have to do the C-Section!"

Apparently that was the baby's cue to make an entrance, because with that one push James was born almost literally flying out of the womb. The doctor literally had to *catch* him, as all six pounds, fourteen ounces of him arrived at 3:48pm. He was covered in a white film — an indication that he was, in fact, premature — and immediately taken by the nurses to be checked out. It was at this point the doctor wanted to know what she was missing from Vicky's chart.

We told her the whole story, and she agreed with us that James was approximately eight weeks early. Unfortunately, she couldn't change our doctor's records and mark him as a premature, but it was good…and God was on the case.

When she was born, Katie had jaundice, which is an unusually high bilirubin count indicating that she took in too much of the stuff during the birth and needed to flush it out of her system. She ended up in the hospital an extra day or two. James' count was much worse, and he was in the hospital several more days as they struggled to get his count down. It was basically a toxin in his system, and at his young age he didn't have the immune system to knock it out. If left untreated, it could become deadly.

Still, I knew my amazing God didn't give us another baby only to take him away from us. So we prayed. It was heartbreaking, because they would only let him out for feedings. The truly heartbreaking portion still lie ahead of us.

When they finally sent James home, they sent him with a home ultraviolet light kit to get his bilirubin count down. This was one of the first types of models of this kind that could be administered at home, and entailed a special cover of lights over his crib with a plastic guard around his neck to protect his head. It looked like a medieval torture device. I would sit there between nursings, holding his hand as he wore the thing, crying both literally and figuratively out to God. "Heal my boy!" After the hospital and now this wrinkle at home, I'd run out of prayers. I was exhausted. I sat holding his hand, tears running down my face, quietly praying in the spirit.

The day eventually arrived when James was finally out of the woods and we could stop putting him in this device. Finally, we could hold him like normal parents. We could cuddle with him, could lay him in our lap or on our arms or sitting together on the couch.

It was fantastic to have our son fully healthy. He did have his night and days mixed up, which extended over Christmas. The company had given me a week vacation, coupled with two additional weeks of shut down, mimicking the government between Christmas and New Year's. Combined with my two weeks of vacation after the first of the year, I was essentially off with James for the first five weeks. As we worked to adjust him to a regular sleeping schedule, I would sit up all night holding him and loving on him, watching re-runs of Babylon 5 together (gotta train them up right). Those became cherished moments for me. Even today, looking at my son as the grown man he's become, I'm reminded of just what a miracle he is and thank God for him.

This is a huge stone in my altar, because of the immense joy I've experienced every day with my son. All of my kids are amazing, and I'm so blessed to have them. Since this time, Vicky and I have spoken to many couples, giving them hope that if God put a desire on their hearts to have kids, it doesn't matter what the world says.

WENT TO THE VIDEO STORE AND GOT AN ENGINEERING JOB

'If you consent and obey, You will eat the best of the land; '
- Isaiah 1:19

September 11, 2001, was a day that will definitely live in infamy. I remember heading to work at a cellular company, hearing the news on the radio. Being from the New York/New Jersey area, I knew what the skyline looked like and what those towers represented. I also knew a plane wouldn't strike the towers by accident unless a huge amount of errors took place, including low cloud cover with inclement weather. When I heard that it was clear skies in New York City, I told Vicky, "This is an attack!"

In addition to this, at the time of the attack I had a family member who worked next to the World Trade Center Twin Towers (tower 1 and tower 2) in one of the additional buildings that collapsed. I'd raced home in hopes of hearing if he was alright, and thankfully he was. His father had come to his apartment early in the morning and took a personal day to spend it with him. This innocuous act might have very well saved his life.

Following the devastation of that September morn, just before the collapse of the financial markets with Enron and Arthur Anderson scandals, I was laid off from my job working on cellular infrastructure in early November. Sadly, it was a job I really had enjoyed. The company had taken a huge financial hit and was downsizing approximately a third of their workforce (around 40,000 employees). Because of this, they were offering a sizable severance package which paid me for six months *and* kept my insurance active for the entire duration. It was basically like getting all of the benefits without any of the work. It was cool for about the first week, and then it grew real old, real fast, and I found myself looking for something to do.

I dabbled with creating some Christian games and sought to start a company to make a business out of it. However, starting a business and pioneering a new market when no one saw the potential *and* you didn't have the start-up cash for it didn't seem like good recipe for success. Instead, the project ended up eating a ton of time and energy, way more than I expected. Soon that "free" severance money began running out.

It was about this time that the financial scandals hit and the telecom bubble (the initial flood of internet developers that created a huge demand for software developers) burst, causing a drastic flip in the market. Suddenly it very, *very* difficult to find a job. It wasn't unusual to show up to an interview and see a line of at least ten other applicants also interviewing for the same position.

I'd squandered the time I had on an endeavor which I never ran past God for His guidance, and now I was in a pickle. I was beginning to really, really worry, enough that I was even applying to work at fast food restaurants and video rental stores, only to be denied because… (wait for it…) I had a college degree. It was beyond frustrating, to say the least.

After being declined for even an interview by my third fast food place, I decided to apply to a video rental store, conveniently leaving off the parts about my degree or any degree-related jobs. Before I knew it, I got an interview… mostly because the manager wanted to hear why I hadn't worked in, like, six years (time in college plus working in the profession). I fumbled an explanation about not being able to get a job, and back then saying I was a stay-at-home dad wasn't a thing.

She saw right through me.

I don't know if it was the way I spoke or the fact that I showed up to the interview in a suit, but she stared me down. "You have a degree, don't you?!"

At this point, being asked so directly, I knew that I had to tell the truth. I'd reasoned leaving it off was an omission instead of an outright lie, which didn't sound bad in my mind. I rationalized it was for my family, after all. But a direct question... well, that needed a direct answer. So I told her that I had an engineering degree, upon which she immediately told me I wouldn't get the job, suspecting I would leave as soon as I got a job in my chosen field.

I told her I would sign an agreement to work for them for at least a year or two, provided she offered me a job I could feed my family with. She wasn't sympathetic to this idea and continued to decline.

Following that disastrous interview, I was completely broken. I had no idea what to do, and feared losing our apartment, not having food and seeing my kids homeless and on the street.

Thank God my wife found a job working as a helper to a mom's day out program. She was only making minimum wage, but at least that meant some income. However, compared to my old engineering salary, it wasn't even close to our rent, let alone food and the rest of our bills.

Still, God was faithful and somehow we survived. This does not mean that we didn't have to struggle to feed our family, because we certainly did. I can remember several times when we didn't have enough food to feed everyone, so my wife and I would just let the kids eat and tell them we were going to go out on a "date" or eat later, or how we were fasting. At the time we thought we were sparing our children the harsh reality we were living in, but we recently discovered they were smart enough to figure it out, despite their young ages.

In Katie's own words, "I realized that all those times you said you were fasting was because we didn't have enough food, and you were making sure we could eat!"

In the middle of this is when we discovered we were pregnant with James (see Here Comes Blessing Number 3).

In the beginning of September, several months after the money from my severance had run out, I was becoming increasingly desperate. I'd just about completely given up on getting a job as a software developer or electrical engineer, and was just looking for absolutely *any* job anyplace that would hire me. Minimum wage, retail, service industry, telemarketing, janitor — whatever, it didn't matter to me. I was shooting out resumés and filling out job applications all over the place, but not getting very many callbacks. I mean, I even applied at Walmart as a stocker and didn't get called back!

I began to think I had the plague or something, as if I would look above me and see Charles Schultz's Pig Pen stink lines hovering overhead. I was running out of options and didn't know what else to do. I spent many, many nights crying out to God, and sometimes even felt like He had utterly abandoned me. The leaders in the church I was in were no help either, as they told me I must be sinning in some way, which was obviously why God wasn't allowing me to get a job. That didn't help. It only made me angrier.

Angry at God.

Angry at God's people.

Angry at the world.

But my anger wasn't helping me get a job any faster, so it was essentially useless. I was lost.

One particular night, however, I'd had enough. I was up in the wee hours of the night that bleed into the very early hours of the next day, and I started yelling at God. After some time venting my pent-up emotions, I moved on to pleading with Him, and later attempted to bargain. Finally, however, I just broke down and cried out.

I remember during the different stages of praying I tried to "trick" God into helping me, stating, "Don't do it for me, but do it for my wife! Do it for my kids, who love You so much!" Obviously, God knew exactly what I was doing and didn't respond to it. I was angry and mad and frustrated and tired and weary and desperate and broken. So very, very broken. But most of all I was confused.

I felt I'd done everything right. I worked hard for the company and lost my job through no fault of my own. I was praying every night and day, I was reading my Bible, being the best supportive husband and father I could be. While I was far from perfect, in my mind I was doing all the right things that I knew to do, and at that moment on that night it had all come to head.

My heart broke. I laid humbly before the Lord, crying. I don't remember why, but for some reason I'd decided to pray until I heard a clear answer from God — no matter how long it took. And there, drowning in my pool of tears, eviscerated and laid bare before God… He answered.

God spoke audibly, saying, "Go to <Christian TV Station>. And I will give you a job today!"

I can't begin to explain how excited I became. In an instant, with just a simple word from God, I was transformed. On cloud nine. I was going to get a job at a Christian television station! This was going to be so absolutely amazing!! I could hardly sleep!

I woke up the next morning with a new sense of purpose and bounce in my step. I cleaned myself up and donned my best dress suit, complete with tie and jacket. I printed off a few copies of my resumé and grabbed a video tape (VHS, dating myself here for sure) containing some home videos and graphics I'd collected. I perused their website looked over the job listings, getting myself more and more excited as the minutes marched forward. God was going to give me a job there! Today!!

I jumped in my car and headed off to the station office. I didn't know if God was going to get me a job using my engineering or programming background or something else like video editor, but I didn't care. All I knew was somehow, in some way, God was getting me a job today.

I arrived at the station, appraising and approving of the building as my new work home, wondering where my cubicle or office would be. I had a strong air of confidence as I entered the building and was greeted by the receptionist.

"Hello," I said, flashing my biggest smile. "My name is Patrick Aquilone, and God sent me here to get a job."

I hear you laughing. (Or is that a groan…?)

Now, looking back on this moment some twenty years later, I find myself laughing. Imagine the gall of this complete stranger, wandering into the lobby and saying such a thing to a poor unsuspecting receptionist, who probably hears this on a weekly basis. But there I was, all proud and with my chest out, expecting her to be like, "Oh, thank God you're here! We've been waiting for your arrival!" and then take me back to start my employment paperwork.

Yes, I was naive and foolish, but I *had* heard a word from God, and I just knew that He was going to give me a job that day.

The receptionist smiled apologetically. "I'm sorry, but we don't have any openings right now. You can go on our website and fill out and application, for when something opens up."

I chuckled at her. "I'm sorry, but *God* sent me."

"Yeah..." the receptionist rebutted, "I heard you... but we don't have any openings."

I leaned over the counter toward her. "I understand," I said, "but you see, God told me to come here and get a job. So if you could just call someone from Human Resources..."

"I'm not calling anyone except security if you don't go ahead and leave." She was cool as a cucumber.

It was at this point I realized she probably got this all the time. The difference was I really *had* heard from God, so in my mind all I needed to do was persuade her. That's when the thought hit me that this must be a test.

Well, I was usually good at taking tests back in college, so I held my ground. I continued, undaunted. "I realize you probably hear this all the time, but God *really did* speak to me last night, and said, 'Go to <Christian Station> and I will give you a job today!"

"Right," the receptionist replied disdainfully. "Perhaps God meant He would give you a job somewhere else...because *we don't have any openings!*"

I was frustrated, yes, but not yet defeated. "If I could just talk to someone in Human Resources..."

"No one is going to want to talk with you!"

I changed tactics, attempting to reason with her. "How about this," I began, "you call Human Resources and just ask. If no one is willing to talk to me, I will leave."

I'm not sure if it was God or my handsome smile or maybe she really wanted to see how this would play out, but to my surprise she agreed and made the call. The person in charge of technical recruiting agreed to speak with me, but only over the phone.

I smiled and thanked her as she routed the call to a courtesy phone in the lobby. I still remember how he started the conversation. "Mr. Aquilone," he began, "I've seen your resume online, and it's impressive. The kind of people we like to hire."

I grinned. This was off to a great start! I could feel the excitement welling up inside me because I just *knew* a miracle was about to happen.

"However," he continued, "I'm sorry to tell you that we just do not have any openings."

"But..." I replied, perplexed. "... God told me to come."

"And I'm absolutely sure he did," added the man, "but maybe this was more about obedience and not a specific job here."

"I'm confused," I admitted.

"I understand. And honestly, if I had anything open I would let you interview, but we just don't. I will mark your resume, and when something opens up you will be the first one we call. Please have a good day!"

With that the man hung up the phone.

In the twenty years since that moment, I've never received a single call from them. Go figure.

I thanked the receptionist and, true to my word, I walked out of the building...feeling deflated and defeated. As I approached my car I ripped off my tie and shouted at God so loud they undoubtedly heard me inside the building.

"I did what you said," I screamed. "Why didn't I get a job?! I don't understand! I was obedient!"

I was more than confused as a fresh storm cloud of depression loomed on the horizon of my mind, preparing to hit me hard. The words fell into my mind like rain, sprinkling me with negativity. "You're such a loser. You will *never* get a job!"

Still, I *knew* God spoke to me the night before, but in that moment *none* of it was making sense. I mean, if I *had* heard from God, then why was I not sitting in an interview right then, discussing a position and getting an offer? And if I *didn't* hear from God (when I was so certain that I did), then how far had I fallen from His grace and His presence that I no longer recognized God's voice?

I was broken, beyond broken. Smashed and shattering into smaller and smaller pieces with every passing second. At that point, I was sitting in my car, once more crying before the Lord. As tears raced down my face, I suddenly realized I had another problem: I couldn't go home.

I'd told my wife — *told my little girls* — that Daddy was coming home with a job that day, because God told me He would give me one. How could I go home now, telling them that not only did I *not* get a job, but that I clearly didn't hear the voice of God?

I couldn't. I just couldn't.

It would shatter what little faith my wife was holding on to at this time. I had to come home with a job, but I clearly had *no clue* how to do that, as I'd been searching hard for months leading up to that point. So I sat in my minivan, deflated and not knowing what to do next.

After some time, I broke down and prayed to God that He would help me, somehow, because as far as I was concerned it was "All *Your* fault! After all, *You* got me into this mess!" Obviously, this wasn't true, but it was genuinely how I felt and I had no trouble telling God all about it.

Eventually, I drove out of the parking lot and got back on the main road. I had no destination in mind, but kind of drove around for a short bit before a new thought entered my head. I fashioned myself a movie buff, maybe I could score a job at one of those video rental stores? In the moment, I completely forgot the previously mentioned interview (and how it most definitely did *not* get me a job). Once this idea got in my head all I could think about was how fitting this would be. I would be talking about movies all day long with people, recommending good ones and maybe even steering families away from bad ones. The biggest perk? Getting to rent new movies *for free*.

It was like a godsend in my mind, and I quickly drove to the nearest video store which, as it happened, wasn't the one I interviewed at earlier. I drove to the store and went in, walking around for a moment, imagining myself working there, and then selected a movie I wanted to see. We really didn't have the money to rent a movie, mind you, but somehow that didn't stop me.

As I approached the counter and was being checked out, I asked if she was the manager. She was, so I asked if they had any positions open.

"We have some part-time associates positions open."

"What about management positions?"

Something inside screamed that I should mention I had a degree, as it might somehow score me a job. This is where my months of job searching should have told me to *leave that part out*. But I wasn't listening or remembering any of that, all I could hear was the nagging voice telling me to let her know I had a degree. "I have a bachelor's degree," I added. "It's in electrical engineering, but I'm sure some of it can apply."

"We usually like to hire from within, and honestly, I'm not aware of any openings."

At this point, a stranger interrupted me from beside us. "Do you really have a degree?"

I looked over at him with wide eyes. I'd never seen this man before in my life. I didn't even see him enter the building. As I'm writing this, I wonder if I actually met an angel that day, as you will see why this could have been in a moment.

I stared at the man, wondering why someone would be so rude, interrupting what I'd felt was my last chance at getting a job to support my family. "Yes," I snarked back at him, then returned my attention to the manager.

The stranger pressed further. "And you have an engineering degree?"

I responded "Yes" again, getting even more upset with guy. I mean, who did he think he was? And why was he suddenly so interested in what degree I had, rudely interrupting my conversation? In that moment, all I wanted to do was strangle the guy and get back to my conversation which, let's be honest, wasn't going so well.

"An engineering degree from an actual college?" continued the stranger.

At this point I really had enough of this guy, and I was ready to take out my full frustration on him. I turned around, giving him my full attention, along with the full intensity of my imagined superhero heat rays beaming out of my eyes to thwart this villain, burning up his puny body.

"Yes," I growled. "I have an electrical engineering degree from Rutgers!" I shot this back as if I was launching a missile strike at some deserving third world power that had just crossed the line for the last time. To be honest, I was so rude, I'm surprised he continued to talk to me at all. But what I *didn't* know was God was in this mix and I was about to be in the middle of a miracle.

"And you need a job..." The stranger was unfazed by my attitude or lack of tact.

"Yes," I replied, "I do."

I turned back to the manager who had excused herself since my rental transaction was complete. I was about to follow her to rekindle the conversation about a job, but again the man interrupted me.

"My mom works for a tech defense contractor," he said, unaffected by my attitude. "They're always looking for good engineers." He then wrote her name, number and email address down on a piece of paper, handed it to me. "Tell my mom that her son sent you, and you need a job." Finishing his last sentence the man left the store.

Honestly, I wasn't sure how to take this. I mean on the one hand I left home telling my wife I wouldn't return until I had a job. On the other hand, this really wasn't the job I set out to get, nor was it a guarantee of a job. Heck, it was only a *contact*.

I was all befuddled as I got in my car and slowly drove home, asking God if this was real and what to do next. I mean, God told me He was going to give me a job at a Christian television station, not a tech company. Didn't He? Or...did He? I decided to go home and try and call the guy's mother.

When I arrived at home I made an immediately beeline for the phone and made the call. She was out on lunch. *Figures*, I thought. I went to my computer and crafted the best email that I could, telling this lady how her son had given me her number and I was available for an interview at her convenience. Then I prayed. I was exceptionally confused by how this day was shaping out to be.

About an hour later, I called the lady again and this time got her at her desk. I introduced myself and mentioned that her son had given me her name and number.

"Where does my son know you from?" she asked.

I reluctantly recounted meeting him at the video store, along with the earlier exchange. She was quiet for a moment and then pressed on, "Are you sure you didn't know my son before today?"

I replied that I didn't, getting worried I had somehow messed up this potential job. She then told me that it doesn't seem possible that I only just met her son today, because she just came from an hour lunch with her son where he spent the entire time talking about me and how her company had to hire me.

I just about dropped the phone and fell off of my chair.

She concluded the call by saying, "Well, now I have to bring you in and at least see this guy my son couldn't stop talking about."

She scheduled an interview, and when I finally did sit down face-to-face with her, things went extremely well. Within two weeks I was offered a job, which I happily accepted.

God was true to His word. I *did* go to the Christian Television station and I *did* get a job. It was just that those two sentences weren't connected as I thought they were. The first was about obedience, which lead to the second, where I got a job because God put it on the heart of a complete stranger to help me out.

It wasn't at all what I'd expected, but I'm very thankful to God for His miraculous way of providing me an engineering job in the middle of a video rental store.

This is a *huge* stone in my altar, because it constantly reminds me that if we follow what God tells us, He will take care of us. Even if it means a stranger will interrupt your carefully-laid plans, just so God can open the door for an interview. Praise God.

FALLING ANGEL

'The Lord heard the voice of Elijah, and the life of the child returned to him and he revived. Then he stretched himself upon the child three times, and called to the Lord and said, "O Lord my God, I pray You, let this child's life return to him." Elijah took the child and brought him down from the upper room into the house and gave him to his mother; and Elijah said, "See, your son is alive." '
- 1 Kings 17:21-23

In the Summer of 2003, James was eighteen months old and growing fast. Katie and Abby had been huge helps for us in raising James, because Vicky and I both worked. In addition, we did a lot of extra stuff for the church and other activities like girls soccer and volleyball. We were a busy but happy family, growing in the Lord — which also made us a prime target for the enemy.

On one particular Sunday, the cowardly yellow bellied slimy creep the devil went after James. He didn't go after my wife. He didn't go after me. Instead, he went after an innocent eighteen-month old. That should tell you all you ever need to know about how evil the enemy is.

On a normal Sunday when my wife was working, I would be engaged with the kids, playing something or watching a movie together. This day I'd been up the entire previous night, feverishly completing a promotional video for some missionaries our church supported. I'd received the final video and photos late on a Friday, and Sunday was the last day they were going to be in the church. This left me little choice but to work through the night. However, I felt that the time was well spent, as the video was going to be used in all the churches which supported them, as well as those considering support of their mission work.

I didn't mind the long hours, I was just really pushing it to get it done and rendered on time. Back then, video production meant a lot of waiting for the computer to render all the frames, especially if you added overlay graphics or text. This project had quite a lot of both. I'd just finished with enough time to give it a final preview and then hit the shower. By the time Sunday after church and lunch rolled around, I'd been up for close to 48 hours straight and was exhausted. I sat down on the couch, put on a movie that all three kids liked, honestly attempted to watch with them but wound up drifting off to sleep.

This passed the torch to keeping an eye on things to my nine-year-old daughter, Katie. I hadn't told her she was in charge or to keep an eye out, because I'd intended on remaining awake. However, I was comfortable enough in her abilities and love for Abby and James to know I could fall asleep.

Everything was fine until Mother Nature gave Katie a call. Since she wasn't specifically told to make sure everyone was safe, the apartment was locked, and Abby was also in the room, she didn't feel there was any concern and went about answering nature's call. (And let's not forget, her Dad was also in the room.)

Abby was deeply engrossed into the movie, unaware I'd fallen asleep or that her big sister had left the room. All she knew was it was family movie time, and she was having a delightful time. So much of a great time, in fact, she didn't even notice when James left the room.

The next part is a bit of speculation from the available facts, based upon knowing my son, but both Vicky and I believe this is either what happened or extremely close.

James decided to follow his big sister Katie and left the living room, crawling down the hall toward the bedrooms. He had obviously missed her going into the bathroom, or maybe he simply decided to go into her bedroom, only she wasn't there. We figure he must have heard a sound or seen something that drew him…to the open second story window.

In this apartment complex the windows were about four feet tall and only six inches from the floor. A lovely effect for lighting the room with natural light, but not great for little children. James crawled over to the window and pressed against the screen, leaning into it to see whatever it was that caught his attention. The screen slowly snapped out from the frame, descending toward the ground with James on its back. (Later that day, we would find the screen on the ground directly below the window.)

From this point forward we are returning to the accurate, first-hand account.

A knock on our door jarred me awake. I opened my eyes to see Abby getting up to answer and to see who it was. I heard our downstairs neighbor frantically describing how she found James crawling out from behind a bush near the back corner of the apartment building, crying and wearing nothing but his diaper.

Instantly, I thought this was a really sick and cruel joke to play on anyone, let alone a parent. That was, until she took a step into the apartment *HOLDING JAMES*!

She was holding my diaper clad baby!

I leapt off the couch and grabbed my son. He wasn't crying or even responsive. I quickly thanked our neighbor and immediately placed James on the floor. Eons ago I'd taken a first responder class and was now utilizing those skills as best as I could remember to do a quick assessment of his condition.

What I saw and felt scared the life out of me.

His eyes were rolled back in his head. His whole body was red. His neck wasn't supporting his head, flopping around limply, causing me to have to keep constant support for it as I checked him. When I lightly pressed on his ribs to assess if there was a break I couldn't find a single solid mass.

My best guess he had shattered his rib cage, making the timing of getting him to the hospital critical before he could bleed out internally.

The worst thing was, although he was still breathing, the only response I could get out of him was barely a whimper as I pressed to feel for missing bones. I was absolutely horrified as I hollered for the phone.

We only had one car at the time, and my wife had taken it to work only an hour earlier. For whatever reason I cannot fathom at this moment, I didn't think of calling 911 for emergency, but instead hyperfocused on how fast I could get my son to the hospital.

Vicky managed a video rental store that had been short staffed, which meant she worked a lot of extra hours, including Sundays. This also meant she might not have the coverage to be able to get off and bring the car to race James to the hospital. Had I been fully lucid and in full control of my senses and emotions, I likely would have called for an ambulance. However, I wasn't thinking straight or rational, in shock that my son had just sustained very possibly fatal injuries.

I can't tell you how much of a failure I felt in that moment. I felt as if my world shattered into a million pieces, and all I wanted to do was beat the ever-loving crap out of the man who was holding the hammer. Only to discover later that man was me.

As broken as I was, I knew I had to get my son to the hospital. In my mind, if I got the car in time he would make it.

My daughters brought me the phone, also freaking out that James might be seriously hurt. I'm sure they didn't know the extent of his injuries or what it meant, but they knew he wasn't acting himself. Later I would find out they each blamed themselves for what happened, even though none of it was their fault. Nor was it James's fault. I'm not even sure that it was my fault, although I totally take the blame. Even if I'd been awake, I might have thought James went with Katie, and everything else would have still happened.

The true villain here is the devil, who found a way to lure my son into a trap so he could attempt to drive a wedge in my family. I thank God he didn't succeed.

I quickly dialed the phone.

Vicky answered, and through my tears and fears I somehow managed to inform her about James falling out of the window.

"HE WHAT?!!"

Immediately anger and dread pierced the air, my wife's volume and tone getting the attention of the entire video store. As her mouth dropped, the assistant manager didn't ask any questions, but simply said, "**GO!**"

Vicky hung up the phone and made it from her work to our front door in mere moments, during which time I was on the phone getting someone to watch the girls. As soon as my wife arrived we were out the door.

It was typically a fifteen-minute drive to the hospital. I made it in under five. Frantically, we rushed into the emergency room and described what had happened. The hospital moved us to the front of the line and quickly took our son into a special examination room.

James was still not responding. It wasn't looking good as the nurses and the doctor made their initial check, then ordered every test that hospital could perform, from x-rays to CAT scans and everything in between.

And yes, I did say scans. Not just one, but a series of many, many tests. They weren't taking any chances and checked *everything*. The events that happened next are honestly kind of a blur, as I went with James from one test apparatus to another. As we were being wheeled around, I felt everyone glaring at us.

I don't know if you have ever been in a situation where no one believed your story, and instead substituted one of their own, but that's what was happening to us. Instead of believing James fell out of a window, they twisted the tale into a dark nightmare, full of torture and horrible abuse of our son. In line with this perceived version of the events, the hospital placed us in an all glass examination room so they could keep an eye on us.

In addition to this, we were hardly ever alone for more than a moment with James as they waited on the results. Now, I understand why the staff responded this way. I'm sure they'd seen their fair share of abused children, and James's story sounded a bit outlandish. Among the evil looks, hushed whispers and self-condemnation, I'd been doing all I could to keep it together...and failing. My innards were full of knots, as tiny, fire-breathing dragons tried to vacate the luxurious accommodations of my stomach.

In the middle of all of this turmoil, I glanced down at my son on the examination table and realized his beautiful brown eyes were staring back at me. I don't know how long they had been open, but they were alert and looking deeply into mine. Tears rushed down my cheeks and I leaned over to hug him.

One of the hardest parts came when they needed to take the scan of his head. In order to get a good image, they had to strap him down so he wouldn't move. Since he was now alert and responsive, he made it clear he didn't like being so confined. He began screaming and crying as the table moved into the machine. In a feeble attempt to try and calm his fears, I stood just outside the scanner and rubbed his foot. I don't know if it helped, because he still screamed, but at least it allowed me to let him know I was still there.

As the machine spun up to take the scan, James stopped screaming and uttered two very distinct words, "DA-DA!"

My heart broke into a million pieces. I wanted to rip him out of there and save him. I screamed out to the technician who had already instructed the machine to pull James back out. I was ready to Hulk out and smash the entire building apart, all while cradling my son in safety.

At least, that's how it would have happened in my mind.

As James emerged from the scanner, I tore through his restraints, not waiting for the technician so I could lift him up and hold him, cuddling him in my arms. It was such a touching moment, not only was I in tears, but also Vicky and the two scanner technicians. I would have walked through an active volcano for any of my children if it meant their health and safety, and I guess the technicians noticed.

Here is where God is awesome. My son became increasingly alert, crying and wanting his Daddy. That should have clicked in our minds that God was healing our son, but it didn't. It wasn't until the doctor bolted into the exam room with a head of steam that we began to understand.

He proceeded to loudly berate us for bringing a perfect healthy baby into the emergency room and wasting all of their time, energy and money. Instantly I was ready for a fight, especially since I knew the condition my son was in when we arrived. Who did that doctor think he was, accusing my son of being healthy?! I was going to give him a good piece of my mind…and possibly my fists.

Cooler heads prevailed, however, and at that moment Vicky walked over and examined James. I joined her, and in awe of God, we assessed James and found none of his original conditions were present. James had his eyes wide open and was alert, his skin had returned to normal color and his ribs cage was firm and solid once again. If that wasn't enough, he was going stir crazy, grabbing everything he could and was playing with it. We had our hands full keeping him away from possibly dangerous items.

The doctor exclaimed he must have landed on a bush and "got lucky," which is why he didn't have any injuries aside from a tiny cut on the top of his head. It was a ludicrous explanation, as James would have had to fly out of the window, banking right as he swung around a three-foot width and one foot deep outcropping, then sailing another good six feet *parallel* to the building only to land gently on the bushes at the corner of our apartment. Plus, he would have had to do all of this without the screen, later found directly under the window.

Our neighbor *did* say she found my son crawling by the bushes, but the physics involved for him to get there wasn't even plausible. I went over and over it again and again, and each time had the same result. I examined the exterior of the building by the window multiple times, and each time came to the same conclusion. Not possible! It wasn't just our word for it, as many of our friends and family later examined that location and also concluded that there is no way my son could ever have made it to the bushes without divine intervention.

We left the hospital with a discharge to follow up with our primary care doctor. I called his office the next morning. The nurse put me on hold and when she came back, she said, "*The doctor wants you to drop whatever you're doing and immediately bring your son into the office!*"

I almost dropped the phone, my heart racing into instant panic mode. When we entered the office building we were immediately taken into the back where our doctor met us in the exam room. The reason for the rush was in the last couple of days he had seen two other children who had taken serious falls. One had fallen out of a shopping cart and cracked their skull, while the second had fallen out of a first story window on grass, and now needed cosmetic surgery. He was convinced the emergency room doctor had missed something.

He thoroughly — *thoroughly* — examined my son, turned to us and said, "Count your blessings!" He then went on to explain to us exactly how powerful of a miracle this was.

As if this wasn't enough, we had something else happen within all of this that confirmed for us God was involved in protecting and healing my son. Following the hospital and doctor's visit, James began crawling around saying the word "Nana." He had never said that word before, nor were any of us trying to teach him this word. When he would say that word, he would be crawling around from room to room or around corners or obstacles, as if he were searching for something or someone.

Nana was the name my mother asked the grandkids to call her, which isn't necessarily unusual…except for the fact that my mother had passed away *almost five years prior* to James being born. It's our firm belief that God had my mother catch my son that day, which is why he kept looking for Nana afterwards.

This is a huge stone in my altar because it underscored exactly how much both I and God love my son. I love my kids and would do anything for them. To see any of them hurting breaks me in ways I never thought possible. For God to heal my son so there was no permanent damage to his body or mind made me forever thankful, and it forever reminds me that God truly does love the little children.

GOBBLE, GOBBLE, GOBBLE...GOBBLE

'For thus says the Lord God of Israel, 'The bowl of flour shall not be exhausted, nor shall the jar of oil be empty, until the day that the Lord sends rain on the face of the earth.' So she went and did according to the word of Elijah, and she and he and her household ate for many days.'
- 1 Kings 17:14-15

2005 was a year that rocked my world — and especially my view on my finances. Up until that point I had come to believe God wasn't in the mix when it came to giving to a church or ministry. Back when I was around seven or eight, I found my grandfather's offering envelopes at his house. The church had them pre-printed, complete with a specific amount on them. As a kid, I concluded the church he attended had imposed or forced him to give that amount — or else. This was further strengthened by some of the stories (which I later learned were just that, *stories*) my father would tell me about the church and their forcing our Italian family to give large amounts of money — or else we wouldn't be allowed to be members *or* blessed.

Today, I recognize the envelopes were because he had given a commitment to the church with the amount already set, so he couldn't rationalize himself out of giving in the future (and through which, I might point out, he was super, super blessed for). So it was somewhat of an understatement to say my view of giving and tithing was skewed.

During the summer of 2005, God spoke to me about giving a large amount, and when I followed through He blessed me amazingly from it. It was uncomfortable and exhilarating, shaking my foundational ideas of money, of God and giving. I was happy and surprised. Excited and perpetually perplexed. What I had experienced didn't connect with what I'd grown to believe. Still, God wasn't done with me yet.

On the Sunday before Thanksgiving 2005, I was struggling. Since early summer I'd been giving faithfully, but my heart wasn't really into it. I was doing it because God had blessed me before, but I felt if I stopped the blessings would also stop, as if God would somehow stop loving me. (This isn't true, of course, but that's how I felt.) However, leading up to this Sunday I'd been working as a contractor, which meant when the money for contractors waned, the amount of hours I could work was reduced.

I was working for a defense contractor company who went by a calendar year, meaning they wound down their budgets heading into December. This meant as we got closer and close to the end of the year, I worked less and less hours and made less and less money. In the six weeks leading up to the Sunday before Thanksgiving, I'd worked the equivalent of eight days (if I worked as a full-time employee, it would have been 30 days). This all meant very little money was coming in so little that we didn't have enough to pay any bills or feed our family.

Back to Sunday morning before Thanksgiving. I was sitting on the edge of my bed, arguing with the Lord. The topic? Tithing. I held in my hand the tithe check, representing the remaining money in our account after paying for water and utilities, and still we were negative. I felt God was disconnecting with us and not blessing or loving us anymore, which didn't make sense because up to this check I had been tithing regularly. I was doing exactly what I felt God wanted me to do!

So there I sat, arguing. The last thing I told God before I left for church was, "God I'm going to go to church today and hand in my tithe check. I'm not going to say a word about where we are or our struggles. If you want me to continue to tithe, then you'll have to put it on someone else's heart to reach out to me!"

Pfft. As if God is moved or threatened by ultimatums. But gave God one, right then and there. I thought about King Nebuchadnezzar in Daniel, chapter 2, when he wouldn't share his dream but demanded an interpretation. I wanted to see God move, not just someone's heartfelt compassion or pity. I didn't want to be deceived by kind hearts and words, but really wanted to see the heart of God. So I made this statement to God and headed to church.

True to my word, I didn't tell anyone about the war going on in my mind or the struggle in our finances. Instead, I went to church like nothing was wrong and handed in my check. The only person who knew was Vicky. Interestingly, while I didn't share my thoughts with her, she wasn't telling anyone, either. While I know there are a lot of accounts of people bargaining with God or making deals with God, do you really want to know what I was doing?

It was all about pride.

True, I *did* want to see the heart of God, but a large part of me didn't want others to see I couldn't support my own family, financially. I didn't want to risk others looking down on me. I was afraid they would have seen me as weak, and where I grew up that was unacceptable. So instead of relying on God, I was really relying on preserving my pride.

This irrational and unsupported fear was just plain poppycock. Had we shared, our fellow brothers and sisters in Christ would likely have prayed for us and stood alongside us to see what God was going to do. Praise God, He was (and is) bigger than my pride.

At the end of church after I'd already handed in my tithe, the pastor came over to me. "Could you use a turkey?" he asked me, then went on to explain how the church had purchased some turkeys to give out, but (for some reason that I do not remember) they didn't get to give them away as intended.

Immediately I told him yes, but didn't tell him anything more. He then informed me that someone would be in touch with me later in the day. I waited the rest of the day at home, but no one called. I was disappointed, but chalked it up to either the pastor forgetting or God giving it to someone else in need.

Tuesday evening, and my family and I sat down to literally eat the last meal — the last bit of food we had left. My wife and I exchanged knowing glances, but there wasn't anything else we could do. When we were done eating that night, there was going to be no food left in the house.

Now, you might be thinking "Aren't there food shelves or social services in your area?" Yes, there are... but we made too much money and hadn't gone long enough without a regular income for them to help, so we were no longer eligible. Boggles the mind, sure, but that's where we were at with that.

As for food shelves, you could only go once a week and we had already gone that week to get the food we had. We could go again on Saturday, but that would have left Wednesday through Friday with empty cupboards and stomachs. We could have reached out and asked for help and food from people we knew, but it would have required humility, and I struggled with that. I might have gotten there, come Wednesday morning, but God had something else in mind.

As I sat there with my three amazing kids, tears came to my eyes. I had to choke them back, because the kids couldn't see how Mom and Dad were struggling. Why not? Pride again. I concluded there were some things kids should not be burdened or concerned about. However, they could have been standing with us in prayer that God would provide, because we *were* being obedient. They could have been involved in helping to raise our faith as we walked this out, because the faith of child just believes. I'd let pride rob myself of their support, while simultaneously robbing them of the blessing and encouragement through answered prayer.

As we finished up dinner, the phone rang. It was Hector, the church drummer. After introducing himself, he said pastor had talked to him about getting us a turkey on Sunday and he had completely forgotten about it. "You still want that turkey?" he asked.

"Absolutely," I said.

Then he said something that floored me, words I'll never forget. "Do you by chance want *three* turkeys?"

I'd been trying to figure out how far a single turkey could last when he'd offered the first one. My jaw dropped, and Vicky asked what was wrong while I was motioning to her to wait. I told him that we could, indeed, use three turkeys, and agreed to meet him at the church in a half hour. I put the phone down and quickly shared what Hector had said before racing out the door.

When I arrived at church, Hector was there with his truck open. At this point, I was so humbled by God and His divine providence that I blurted out our situation and how he was a direct answer to prayer, an instrument of God. He teared up, then shared how they came about having three turkeys.

"My wife doesn't like turkey," he said. "But every time she went to _____ and spent $50, they gave her a free turkey. She said God told her someone would need it, so she just kept grabbing them." He shrugged. "So we had these three turkeys in our freezer and Thanksgiving was just a few days away when pastor talked to us about giving one to you. When we were on the phone, I just felt led to ask if you wanted all three."

We hugged and I thanked him profusely because the smallest — the *SMALLEST* — turkey was *twenty-six pounds*.

You read that right. **26 pounds.** The *smallest*.

I drove home praising God the entire time… but He wasn't done with me yet.

When I arrived home Vicky met me at the car to carry in the turkeys. "You are never gonna believe what happened," she said.

"Wait, what?" I was still wrapping my head around what just happened. She continued. While I was gone, a lady from our church who worked for a local television ministry called. They had turkeys to give out to needy families and God put us on her heart, so she was calling to ask if she could come over and drop it off.

She didn't just drop off a turkey, however — she dropped off an entire thanksgiving dinner, complete with all the fixings and desserts and everything, each item in abundance. We had literally gone from empty cupboards to overflowing in less than an hour! We ended up with four turkeys and a ton of sides, enough to easily last the five of us until my next paycheck. We had turkey, turkey sandwiches, turkey and gravy over biscuits, and so much more. We never had so much turkey in our lives, and I was thankful for every single bite.

That night I thanked God beyond words, sitting there weeping and worshipping in awe of Him. I also made the commitment that I would always tithe and I would give when and where He told me to, and He has never let me down. We have never been without a roof over our heads and food in our cupboards. There were still times that looked bleak, of course, but God has always come through.

Thankfully, God continued to work on my pride issues. I'm not sure I've completely won the war yet, but I win far more battles now than I did before this miracle happened.

This is a sizable stone in my altar, because it constantly reminds us if we follow what God says about our money and tithe, He will never let us go without. He will literally open the windows of heaven and fill our cupboards of need — sometimes within the hour. I'm so thankful to God for His amazing blessings.

HOMELESS HUNGRY GOD BLESS

'He who is generous will be blessed,
For he gives some of his food to the poor.'
- Proverbs 22:9

Continuing on the events of 2005, it was the week following Christmas and God had worked it out so I was now getting hours at the defense company I was contracting at. I was in a contract-to-hire position that had yet to be converted over, and I really needed to become an employee so I could have a steady income. I needed the health insurance, especially with three kiddos. I needed to give my wife some semblance of security that we would never become homeless again. It was critically important to move to the hiring portion of the contract-to-hire job.

Up to that point I'd been promised if I'd done a good enough job, they would hire me on as a regular employee — complete with the benefits I needed. As we approached the end of the year, however this hadn't happened, despite my outstanding performance reviews. I was growing uncertain of what the future held, whether I was supposed to stay there or look for employment elsewhere. I prayed constantly, desperate to hear what God wanted me to do.

Just before Christmas, one of the people from our Binghamton, NY location mentioned their location was hiring. She emphasized they were growing desperate for people. The area had suffered from economic issues with major companies closing up shop, which made it hard to come by talented individuals. My experience, coupled with my glowing reviews from teammates in Texas, made her confident I was a shoe in to get hired.

I really didn't want to move, however, because we loved it in Texas. Still, my job search efforts outside of the company had only afforded me one interview, and no offer. So my wife and I prayed and decided I should toss my resumé to the hiring manager, another lady I'd worked with remotely, and see what happened. I don't think she had my resumé for five minutes before she reached out and spoke to my immediate supervisor. After hearing nothing but good things about me, she reached out and we did a phone interview later that same day.

She was impressed and wanted to arrange a face-to-face interview. It felt good to have someone recognize my work who was also in a position to hire me. She'd been planning to come down to the Texas location on another matter in the near future, and could speak with me then. However, I had a counter proposal.

Christmas is a big time for my family, not only for the gifts, but for the feeling of love in air. Since we lived in Texas and the closest family was around sixteen hundred miles away, we infrequently spent any time together with my extended family — let alone any of the holidays — simply because travel was so expensive. Some of our extended family had raised enough money for my entire family to fly up and visit for the holidays. This would be one of our best Christmases with the family and one of the last with my grandparents. Because the plans were set and the tickets purchased, I offered to make the three-hour drive from New Jersey to Binghamton and meet for the interview. The manager agreed, especially since I would also be able to interview with several people that I would be working closely with if I got the job.

At this point, we had lived in Texas for over five years and were uncertain about the possibility of moving back up north. I was very interested in the chance to be closer to family. Secretly I'd hoped they would all discover how great living in the south (i.e., living in Texas) was, and follow us down, but as of the time of this writing it hasn't happened yet.

I was praying a lot because I didn't want to miss God in all of this. My wife, on the other hand, was so convinced by this point that the job was mine and we were moving back to New York, she pulled the kids out of school. She was planning on leaving them in New York with her family as we returned to pack up and move. When the time came, we loaded up the family and were soaring across the northeastern United States.

Our visit with family was fantastic. There was one amazing moment when my son opened up a Christmas gift from my brother-in-law to reveal a giant red fire engine. Upon seeing it was a fire truck, three-year old James stood up and announced, "This is exactly what I always wanted!" Everyone laughed. We split our time between my side of the family and my wife's side. The trip was almost two weeks long, but when you've been away from family for so long, even two weeks feels too short. We decided to tell everyone about the job in Binghamton and how we would be moving back into driving distance, and they were all super excited, as you could imagine.

Before I knew it, the 2nd of January had rolled around and it was time to make the three-hour trek to Binghamton for my interview. I was thankful it wasn't snowing, as the drive there and back was going to be exhausting enough. Since my father had always taught me "to be early was to be on time" and "to be on time was late" when it came to job interviews, I left my grandparent's house just before six in the morning. giving me a little over four hours to make the three-hour drive.

As it was early morning and I was going to opposite way of traffic, I made fantastic time. In fact, I was so early I soon realized I could kill a bunch of time and *still* arrive at the interview early. Soon I had a brilliant idea. Truly brilliant. I mean, it was *epic*.

I recalled a previous visit to Binghamton when some friends introduced me to one of the most amazing pizzas I've ever had the pleasure of eating. The reason it was so amazing was because it was made with Speedie Chicken. Speedie sauce was a marinade that was only available in the greater Binghamton area. They would marinade the chicken over forty-eight hours, grill it and put it on the pizza. It was out of this world.

So, with plenty of time to kill an extra hour before I had to be at the interview, I followed my brilliant idea to drive around and search for the amazing pizza place. I would find it, eat a quick lunch and take off. Easy pizza.

You have to understand, this was long before GPS on our smart-phones, so trying to locate a place was a lot harder. Yes, I decided to drive somewhere I didn't know, with no consideration of how long it would take to get there. All I was thinking about was I had an hour and I wanted to experience that truly amazing pizza one more time. Great plan. (I hope you can feel the sarcasm there).

So off I went, and let me just say this: Binghamton is *not* a small place. I soon became lost. As a typical, red-blooded American man, did I stop for directions? Heck no! I knew exactly how lost I was, and didn't need someone else to tell me. Instead, I was convinced that at any moment something would look familiar… if I just kept driving.

It was about thirty minutes to the hour when I decided I needed to give up on finding my pizza paradise and pursue the interview again. Only one problem: you can't drive to a location if you do not know where you are. I had *no idea* where I was. I reasoned that I'd been basically traveling west, so if I turned around and kept the sun in front of me, *eventually* I would run into the interstate again.

Seemed logical.

Honestly, I was hoping something would either jog my memory or a sign would suddenly appear that read, "Pat! Go this way!" Oh, and you can bet I was praying at this point. Pretty hard.

Eventually, I happened on an intersection with a stop light. Straight across on the other side of the light, a sign informed me the industrial complex area I needed to go to was about fifteen miles ahead. This would be happy news… if the fifteen miles were *on an interstate*. However, this sign was on a city, residential-like area.

It was 9:40AM. My interview was at 10 AM, and the place was

fifteen — FIFTEEN! — miles away. On a road whose currently posted speed limit was 30 miles per hour.

Translation? There was no humanly way possible to make it to my interview on time.

I began to freak out and panic. In my frenzy as I was looking around, I noticed a man on the corner holding a small sign which read, "Homeless, Hungry, God Bless!"

The homeless man wasn't dressed for the conditions. It was almost so cold that it wouldn't have been able to snow, and this man was in jeans, a T-shirt and a greenish wind breaker jacket on over the top. He covered his hands with cloth gloves that had the fingertips cut out. He had scraggly hair and an unkept beard, and I could see his breath expelled from his body as he was shivering.

My heart broke for the man and his plight. I wished I could help, but rationalized I knew nothing of the area and really hadn't anything to offer him. The problem was I could feel the Holy Spirit nudging me to stop and pray for him.

Well, being the blood-bought, Bible-believing, Jesus-loving, Spirit-filled, born again Christian that I was, when the light changed I hit the gas and drove off down the street on my merry way. "I just can't. I have a very important job interview," I said out loud, trying to make myself feel better about leaving him and excuse myself from what God was calling me to do.

I don't know if you have ever heard the audible voice of God, but it isn't all it's cracked up to be, while simultaneously wrapped up in the most amazing experience you could ever have. There were two things happening to me in the moment. The first was what happens whenever the divine invades our physical world, there is just this awe-inspiring, immense, pervasive, immersive *feeling* that floods the air around you energizing it while almost sucking it out, like you were in a giant vacuum bubble but somehow still able to breath.

It's hard to explain but suffice it to say it's a feeling of knowing that you know that you're encountering the otherworldly and divine all at the same time. The feeling you're encountering the living God, the Creator of the universe, right there in the moment and your space (which for me was in the front seat of a minivan).

The second item may be just my personal experience, but the few times God has chosen to speak to me was to rebuke me about something, making the moment extremely bittersweet. If you think your father or mother yelling at you is bad, imagine that… then multiply that a thousand times over. Then multiplied again by a billion millions (kajillion?) and you start to scratch the surface of what it's like to have God rebuke you out loud.

Don't get me wrong, this isn't because God *makes* you feel this way, it's just being in His awesomely holy and pure presence shines a giant light on your lack of purity, pinpointing your sin so there is no hiding. Anyone who thinks they can get away with sin before a living God has never truly encountered him.

The whole time this is happening, there's a huge jumbling, swirling, twirling sea of emotions swimming in the pit of your stomach, a sensation that's both awesome and nauseating. This is your spirit and your flesh at odds. Your spirit's bringing forth your sin so you can repent, while your flesh is feeling conviction and wants to run. Despite this, you're the most excited and full of peace you have ever been in your life.

Obviously, it's a hard feeling to explain this moment, but suffice it to say it's not all butterflies and rainbows (or at least it hasn't been for me). But then, God says those whom He loves, He disciples (Hebrews 12:6), and I was about to receive some discipline in one of the most loving ways. (Note: there is also a very good chance my encounters with the Almighty have been this way because I can be… hard-headed… at times. Fortunately, God really, really loves me.)

I'd made it maybe a mile down the road, laying out my logical and rational case for not being able to stop or even pray with this homeless man — a case which revolved around my all-important interview I was going to be late for. *That* was the moment God shattered the air around me with one question, "Are you ready to be serious, or are you going to keep playing at this God thing?"

OUCH! Double OUCH! Triple Dog Down, Divinely-Inspired OUCH!

Playing at this God thing?

Who did He think I was? Was I really that selfish as to ignore the will of God?

'Playing at this God thing'?

Those words still hit me today, sink into my core as a reminder and a warning. I'd been so wrapped up in what I was expecting or planning or wanting, I hadn't stopped to find out what God wanted — even though I *clearly* heard the Holy Spirit urge my spirit to pray for the man at the corner. The clear sign that He wanted me to minister to that man? I was bolting like a child who doesn't want to take a bath. Just like when Jonah didn't want to go to Nineveh.

I was immediately convicted of my inaction and turned the car around, repenting the whole trip back to the stoplight. I saw the man still standing holding his sign, and pulled into the parking lot. I was reminded of my interview at 10a.m. as I glanced at the clock and noted the time being 9:45a.m. Quietly, I prayed to God, "You're just going to have to handle this!"

I had half a dozen, chocolate-covered donuts and a twenty-dollar bill I felt God telling me to give the man. I slowly walked toward him, feeling like crap inside for what I'd done. He was obviously in need, and my meager offering didn't seem near enough, but it was all I had I could give. As he turned to see me coming, I introduced myself and told him I needed to apologize.

I explained how I was at the stoplight five minutes ago when God told me to stop and pray for him, but instead I just drove on, ready to go on with my day. I informed him how God spoke to me and instructed me to come back and give him the food and the money. He was almost in tears. "I told God ten minutes ago if He was real, He'd better show up!"

Instantly, my heart stopped. Everything became crystal clear, and knew that I knew that I knew that in that moment I was exactly where God wanted me to be, doing what God wanted me to be doing, reaching out in love to this man. I no longer cared about the interview or the drive or anything else, other than knowing I was doing my heavenly Father's will and making Him happy.

It's amazing how, in moments like those, everything else melts away. I didn't even see the cars. I just saw the man and the God who loved us both, and my spirit soared.

I have no idea how long I stood there and spoke and prayed with the man, but it could have been forever and it wouldn't have been long enough. When our conversation was winding down, I began to feel bad that I had no idea where there were any shelters or churches or any place I could take him for more help. He wasn't upset, however, just grateful for the things I gave him. I now understand that moment when Peter said, "*I do not possess silver and gold, but what I do have I give to you!*" (Acts 2:6)

I said one last prayer and bid the man goodbye, wishing I could have done more. I got back into the car, turned the key, heard the roaring of the engine and looked down at the clock, expecting it to be well past 10a.m.

I almost fell out of the van.

I must have been with this gentleman *at least* fifteen or twenty minutes, possibly more. However, when I looked at the clock it still read 9:45a.m. — no time had passed while I was there. None!

In addition to this, I drove the fifteen miles to the industrial area for the interview, still going thirty miles an hour, and arrived with *five minutes to spare*. Again, I'm an engineer and extremely good at mathematical calculations, and there simply is no physical way I could have traveled that distance in that time at that speed.

It was a miracle.

In addition to this, my body was racing like it had run seventeen marathons in record-breaking time, yet I was still as calm and peaceful as a warm summer day, basking lazily in a field, staring at the deep blue sky. I was higher than a kite, on cloud nine. It was the greatest feeling I'd ever experienced in my life… and the day wasn't over yet.

I walked into the building and introduced myself. In all, I spoke with four different people about the potential job, and each and every one of those interviews was… strange. What I mean by "strange" is *none* of them asked me any technical questions, instead talking about an upcoming company picnic, their families or asking me about mine.

Nothing about the job *at all*.

Normally I would have been confused and possibly thrown off my game by this, but I was on such a high from my encounter with the Almighty that I was happy to go with the flow. I left the office feeling as if my feet weren't touching the ground and drove to the nearest Wendy's to call Vicky on a payphone.

When I got her on the line, she immediately wanted to know how the interview went. I told her, "Forget the interview"! You probably could have heard a pin drop on the other end, but I was so bubbling over I couldn't wait. "You are never going to believe what happened to me here after I got lost!" And

Then I proceeded to tell my wife about God and the man and how time had stopped. She was uncharacteristically quiet. When I wrapped up recounting the events, she simply inquired, "But what about the interview?" I then told her all about the interview, puzzling her as much as it puzzled me. Either way, it was over, and whatever God wanted I was totally good with.

A little over three hours later, I arrived back at my grandparent's house. After being greeted by my wife, she informed me I had received a message to call my manager in Texas. I asked her to clarify if she meant the manager from New York or the one from Texas, and she clearly stated my current manager in Texas had been looking for me and it was extremely important I called him as soon as I got back.

I was confused, because I didn't leave my grandfather's number with him or anyone in Texas, for that matter. I grabbed the phone and gave him a call. Apologetically, he immediately offered me a full-time, permanent position with the company, at a salary that included a $20k raise *and* the choice of working in New York *or* Texas.

Immediately, I thought back to the $20 I gave the homeless man, and now I was being offered a $20k raise. I knew it wasn't a coincidence. After speaking with my wife, I accepted the offer to remain in Texas, choosing not to uproot my family. Of course, we were going to have to re-enroll our kids in their elementary schools.

A few days later when I returned to the Texas office, the manager from Binghamton was there and apologized for missing me at the interview (she had been called to fly down the day before). In the course of our conversation, she asked me, "If you don't mind, could you tell me what cologne you were wearing to the interview?"

Cologne? What a strange question.

I told her that I don't generally wear cologne because it irritated my nostrils (something God healed me of somewhere along the way because it doesn't do that anymore). Then I inquired why she was asking me such an odd question. She replied, "Because all four of the guys who interviewed you said the same thing. As soon as they walked into the room, they knew we had to hire you!" Suddenly I knew what the scriptures talk about in Exodus 34 where it showed on Moses's face after he had been encountering God. I didn't know what to say, to that other than to thank her for the interview and helping to get me hired on.

This is a colossal stone in my altar because of two amazing things. First, I heard the incredible, audible voice of God. The fact that it was a rebuke is immaterial to having had the experience. Second, I was walking in the middle of a miracle God was performing. I've no idea what happened to that man or if he was a man or an angel. All I know is I was right in the center of God's miraculous moving hand, and it was an amazing experience.

JAMES AND THE SUV

'The angel of the Lord encamps
around those who fear Him, and rescues them.'
- Psalms 34:7

Roughly in the summer of 2006, we were serving at a church located in an L-shaped strip mall. It was in the corner of a shopping center, surrounded by several other businesses, most of which weren't open on Sunday. One that was open on Sundays, however, was a donut shop. Normally, this donut place would be closed by the time service was over. However, the shop would wisely choose to stay open late, selling half-priced donuts to the churchgoers.

I don't need to tell you how much kids love donuts, *especially* mine. They *loved* going and getting donuts after church. Since it was within the same shopping center, coupled with the fact Katie was almost ten years old, we often let her escort her sister and brother down to get a donut or two.

As we already established, God loves my son James and has helped to keep him from harm (and save his life) on more than one occasion (see Here Comes Blessing Number 3 and Falling Angel). James wasn't quite four years old, loved church and then going with his sisters to get some donuts. The idea for us was the snack would help to tide our children over, because at the time we were bringing several other children to church with us, and due to our limited car size had to make multiple trips. The donut helped the kids (mostly James who didn't fully understand yet) hold out until we were all home and had lunch together.

So it was a normal Sunday, and we handed the kids some money to head down and have their weekly donut fix. The church was positioned at an angle, with the lobby spanning the storefront, looking out onto the parking lot. From there we could see the donut shop, although some cars obscured the exact path and entrance, allowing us to be able to still keep tabs on our kids as they made the track down and back.

This particular Sunday the kids went on their way and Vicky and I were in the lobby talking with other members of the church, both us oblivious to what was about to happen.

I'm not sure if I'd looked down at something like a bulletin or maybe my shoes, but when my gaze returned upright and I looked out at the parking lot, I saw a parent's worst nightmare — *definitely one of my worst nightmares*! James had darted out between two cars, *straight into the parking lot.* His racing out was certainly a disconcerting issue, and one we would have disciplined him for later, but there was a much more pressing issue unfolding. Careening around the corner of the building at high speed, in an obvious effort to bypass the light at the corner, an SUV was gunning it, heading directly for James.

I've heard people say when traumatic events occur, everything slows down, as if you're stuck in a movie, watching all the events unfold with a feeling of helplessness and dread. This was one of the moments.

I watched James as he slowly bounced across the parking lot, not a care in the world. I saw the SUV peeling its tires, horrified as it lined up to hit my son, like a bowling ball finding its mark and taking out that single remaining pin.

I was completely frozen. There was nothing I could do but watch what would most likely be the death of my only son. I remember my mind screaming at my body, "MOVE!" while nothing happened. I wanted to do something — *anything* — to save my son, but this truck was way too close and moving far too fast. I had no chance of even getting through the church doors in time, let alone into the parking lot.

At this point, tears started racing down my face as the realization slapped me hard: I was about to lose my son. And then my horrific nightmare doubled. Racing out from the front of the donut shop shot Katie. She was determined to save her little brother, and with no thought for her own safety darted toward him. (It's also possible she didn't want to hear from Mom and Dad the "How could you let this happen?" inquisitions later.)

Whatever the reason, I watched as she ran out to catch her brother and save him from the monster vehicle rapidly bearing down on his position. Sensing the truck was too close to get away, she heroically wrapped herself around him, almost completely enveloping him, back to the SUV, closing her eyes and preparing for impact.

"NO!" I wanted to scream.

The pastor's wife beat me to it, and let out an extremely loud gasp, causing everyone in the lobby to simultaneously look into the parking lot. And that's when God decided this had gone far enough.

I don't know if it was one angel or twelve, or the fist of God himself, but the truck didn't hit my children. We all watched as the SUV abruptly stopped its forward movement, pivoting upward on the front wheels, kicking the back end into the air behind it. From my vantage point, it looked as if the vehicle went completely vertical. Picture a Hulk sized angel, suddenly and violently smashing both hands down on the front of the hood, the back end flipping up as the front comes to an immediate halt. The SUV's rear portion lifted into the air before plopping back down to the ground.

My two babies were completely unharmed.

The slow motion stopped, and I ran outside and grabbed my children, giving them the biggest hugs I think I've ever given them. Vicky was right behind me with her series of hugs, as the people in the lobby poured out into the parking lot. It was at this point the lady driver of the SUV got out of the vehicle.

She looked in shock and then shocked everyone present when she exclaimed, "I never saw them! I never took my foot off the gas! I've no idea how my truck just stopped!"

She had never let off of the gas!

The only way that vehicle stopped that day was by the miraculous hand of God, supernaturally shielding our children. Thank you, God!!

This is a huge stone in my altar, showing me the miraculous lengths God is willing to go to in order to protect my family. I'm forever thankful to God for this day. I can't tell you why God is so good to any of us, because we certainly do not deserve it, but He is amazingly, awesomely good. Praise God.

THE GANG AND THE TOW TRUCK

'For the equipping of the saints for the work of service,
to the building up of the body of Christ; until we all attain to the unity of the
faith, and of the knowledge of the Son of God, to a mature man,
to the measure of the stature which belongs to the fullness of Christ.'
- Ephesians 4:12-13

Several years ago I was part of a church plant where the initial congregation was around thirty people. The pastor was working as a computer tech, became saved, heard the call to ministry and dropped everything to go to Bible college. After graduating, he set out to plant this church. His real gift or anointing was that of an evangelist. In fact, I believe he held the office of the pastor described in Ephesians 4.

Let me give you an example. The pastor I'm referring to had done a similar style event more than once while I was with him. He would announce on a Wednesday night that we were going to have an outreach on Saturday. This outreach would have us set up at a location (such as the parking lot of the church building) and provide a series of items to the public, such as food, music, and a God-given word.

The congregation would then scramble from Wednesday night to Saturday to make it happen, working out details such as who would cook and serve the food, what music would be played and how would we set up the sound system. Would there be any additional items, such as a skit or dance? Oh, and there would need to be a platform of some kind set up. And drinks… don't forget the need for refreshing beverages.

Now, keep in mind, we were a *super small church plant*, yet the pastor wanted us to have enough food and drink for at least a hundred to several hundred people. It was impressive how this would always manage to come together all the time, and just in the nick of it. Then we would host the event, usually without any advertising at all. No social media. No newspaper ads. Nothing except maybe the thirty of us mentioning to or friends about the event.

Saturday would arrive and it would look like the event was going to be an absolute flop… until about fifteen minutes before the start time. Then, out of nowhere, people would show up! And when I say people showed up, I mean *in the hundreds*. There were times we were very close to running out of food! One time a Christian motorcycle club that rides around and prays over the city happened by. They then called all of their biker friends to attend.

Now, all of this would be impressive by themselves, but the real kicker was when the pastor would get up and preach a message about Jesus and around two thirds of the crowd would give their lives to Jesus. Remember, these were people who weren't coming because it was a Christian event or because they saw an ad. They were pulled by the Holy Spirit at that moment in time to come to a place where they could meet Jesus. This happened more than once. *This* is why I say this pastor held the office of the evangelist.

I will never forget one particular outreach. The pastor had felt a calling to minister to the people who lived in government housing complexes. Since we live in the middle of two major cities, there were plenty of these types of neighborhoods, and Vicky and I had even lived in one many years before in upstate New York. So I was super excited about going out and praying for people and helping to meet their needs. Since I'd seen God meet mine.

The plan was simple. We broke up into teams of two or three and went door to door, asking if the people who answered had any prayer requests. If they did, we would pray for whatever they asked us to, right then and there. If the opportunity presented itself, we would ask them if they knew Jesus and if not, offer to introduce them. If not, we would just thank them for their time and move on. Simple and easy.

It wasn't rare to come across people who needed Jesus and have the chance to pray with them. I believe this was because the pastor heard from God that many were ready, and sent us to reach them.

I was paired up with a man who had spent many years in prison, and as such was very familiar with gangs and gang activity. He was an amazing man of God who had given his life to Jesus and had the humblest spirit, the kind that just oozes Jesus wherever he was, making you wanting to always be around him.

We were assigned a specific set of buildings and had begun our walk. As we had completed our second building and were walking down the street across two parking lots, we caught the attention of four young individuals who began walking towards us. Sadly, they looked like stereotypical, straight out of the movies gang members. They had on red bandanas, wife beater white shirts, ripped jeans and a few leathers straps, chains and were carrying fairly large knives. Everything about them, from their walk to their looks to their mannerisms, all screamed, "Hoodlums!"

I looked over at my partner, who had become literally as pale as a ghost (which was quite the feat for an African American). He stopped in his tracks, grabbed my arm, and said, "Pat, let's head back!"

I turned to him and inquired, "Why?"

"Because they're gang members," he mumbled, "and we're on their turf

He stopped walking, and I looked over at him, surprised. I looked back at the group, now about ten feet from us, and smiled at them. I took a step toward them as my partner tried to restrain me. These individuals each stood about six feet tall and were around two hundred and fifty pounds of pure muscle. As they were approaching us, their chests were popped out and you could see they were getting ready for a fight.

The lead guy, the one closest to me, shouted, "Whatcha doing here?!!" Terror suddenly smacked me in the face, and I was now fully aware why my partner had wanted to leave (and why he was pulling so hard on my arm). I almost didn't reply because fear was trying to grip my heart and steal my voice.

After what seemed an eternity, I uttered, "We're here talking about Jesus!" The instant I uttered the name of Jesus, it was as if someone had taken a pin and popped each one of them.

Their chests dropped. Their demeanor softened. I can't be sure, but I think one of them even smiled as they appeared to shrink down to about five and a half feet tall and maybe one hundred and ten pounds, soaking wet.

The leader lowered his voice. "Whatcha wanna say about Jesus?" We told these guys how much Jesus loved them and went to the cross for them. They had lots of questions about how God could love them, and between my partner and I we answered every one of them. After about thirty minutes of talking, they shook our hands, thanked us for coming and walked away.

You could have pushed my partner over with a feather as they walked away from us. After they were clearly out of earshot, he grabbed me by the arm. "You know their leader had his hand on his gun as they walked up to us, right?"

AH, NO!

I never saw a gun. To this day, when I remember that event I still don't recall a gun. My partner insisted there was one, and I believe there was, but the blood of Jesus protected me so much that I didn't even see it, because that gun was never going to be a threat to me.

If that wasn't enough, as all of this was happening a group of people thought it would be funny to call a tow truck and have my car towed away. After I finished with the group above, my partner and I were speaking to a group of elementary kids at a nearby playground. As we were talking, I looked up and saw a flatbed tow truck booking it down the road *with my car on the back.*

He was still in the complex, but going at least twenty miles per hour. This isn't what you want to see when you're ministering to someone. However, the real shock was running *behind* the tow truck — my pastor, the evangelist.

I watched in disbelief as he overtook the truck, almost as if it were standing still. since then, I discovered an average human of descent shape can run at about eight miles per hour. Additionally, I found Olympic sprinters can do a mile in around three minutes, running at about eighteen miles per hour. Even if Olympians can run faster, my pastor wasn't in Olympic shape. He was in good shape, yes, but not a world-class athlete. This means if the truck was going at least say ten miles an hour or greater, he should *not* have been able to catch the truck.

Now, from my vantage point, the truck was booking it. It was faster than any of the cars we had seen go by. There was no physical way my pastor would have caught that truck, but God!! *God* empowered him to not only catch the truck, but be able to jump up on the side of the truck and get the attention of the shocked driver. He told the driver we were there ministering, and car was one of his people sharing Jesus. He kindly asked the man if he would put my car back, and after their talk, the man swung around to where I had parked.

My pastor walked over to where I was, and I was shocked. He wasn't out of breath and didn't have a bead of sweat on him. He told me he had seen the truck come around the bend and simply took off running. I asked him where they were taking my car, like *that* was the question to ask, instead of, "How did you run so fast?!"

"After explaining to the driver what we were doing, he said he didn't want to get in the middle of anything God was doing and was going to put your car back exactly where he found it!"

I walked back to where I parked my car and true to his word, the tow truck driver was returning my car. As I approached, he asked me if it was where I left it, and if not he would personally move it. He also asked me to inspect the car. If anything was wrong, he would personally pay to get it fixed, stating, "I don't want to get between God and anything He is doing!"

Everything was fine because God protected my car. I got in and drove the car over to where our groups had been meeting up at the other end of the projects, figuring I'd better not give the devil a second chance.

This is a stone in my altar for a couple of reasons. First, I never saw the gun. If I had, my flesh might have overtaken my spirit and I don't know what would have happened. However, God divinely invaded my eyes (with my given permission, I would add) and made sure I didn't see it so we could minister to these young men.

Second, I saw my pastor run at superhuman speed. Perhaps an athlete in tip-top shape could have made that same run, wouldn't have been out of breath or sweating. However, my pastor wasn't that athlete (if they exist). Instead, I saw God divinely invade his body (with his permission, I would add) to help save my car from being impounded and costing me an unexpected sum of money.

Lastly, I had the chance to be a part of God's touching those people's lives. Even the ones who thought it was funny to have my car towed heard the driver say he wasn't interfering with God.

God is so good!

HE SHALL NOT DIE

'I will not die, but live, And tell of the works of the Lord .'
- Psalms 118:17

In 2007, I was working for a defense contractor and we were behind schedule. Our team had plans to be heading out to Alabama where the devices we were writing code for were housed, to continue to develop and fix our flight controllers. There was a ton of work which had to be completed *before* we could head out, so I'd worked long days for something like three weeks straight (without a day off). We had already missed the first deadline and had little hope of making the next one, but the company kept pushing us. They kept pressuring us to work longer and longer hours, and the stress was eating me alive.

It was a lot, I just didn't know how it was affecting me on the inside... but I would soon find out.

On Sunday, September 23rd, I'd gone into work after church and was planning on working another late shift. There was an advantage (if you can call it that) to working at night or over the weekend — none of the management team was there to interrupt our work with meetings. I was always surprised how people thought if they held daily meetings on status updates, each taking at least an hour or more out of a developer's day, somehow our productivity would *increase* (and were always shocked when it did not).

So there I was, trying to get our software to the point where it would be ready for our upcoming October trip. If we didn't meet that goal, we were going to have to do it on site, which would extend our stay — and time away from my family. To compound the matter, the software had met the timeline for the original, agreed-upon requirements. However, a few weeks earlier we'd received a slew of additional requirements, without any change in the timeline or due dates. This was further complicated by the fact that the new requirements approximately *quadrupled* the functionality that had already taken us over three months to write.

To say I was stressed was an epic understatement. I was working somewhere around eighty hours a week, desperately trying to get this thing even remotely close to finished before the deadline. Ironically, I wasn't a lead developer, but nonetheless felt the weight of responsibility to get this code ready in time. Thank God they paid overtime, because it definitely helped our bank account. My family was unhappy with me not being home, and my kids began to hate my job.

It tore me apart inside, because I worked hard to get a college degree so I would have a good-paying job specifically so I could spend *more time with* my family. I was providing for them financially, but wasn't around to enjoy it or reap any of the benefits.

I'd been having a terrible headache that started on Friday, September 21st and just wouldn't go away. I was popping 800mg of ibuprofen every four hours, just to function. I would have taken more except I'd been on strict instructions from my doctor to not exceed that dosage. He told me this because headaches would quickly turn into migraines if not nipped in the bud when they started. (Note: God did heal me of migraines and super thankful for that because when I would get those it would drop me to the ground in tears weeping and just wanting the intense pain to go away.)

I didn't get a migraine during these days, which I felt was because of the ibuprofen. However, the headaches were growing more and more severe, and the medicine only took the edge off so I could bear it enough to work. What I didn't know was these headaches weren't because a migraine trying to form, but something else entirely.

Around 8pm on Sunday I was sitting typing on my computer when suddenly I was paralyzed by severe pain, the likes of which I'd never felt before. It shot through the center of my head, as if someone had taken a giant spear and jammed it from just over my right eye to the base of my skull. It was unbearable, and there was no way I could work with it.

Vicky and I only had one car and I'd taken it to work, planning on working a bunch of hours and then returning home in the early morning for a cat nap before returning to work. The pain was so intense, however, that I knew there was no way I could drive. In order to get home, I needed to call my wife and see if she could get someone to drive her *to me* and pick up both the car and me.

I reached for the phone and had a terrible time grabbing it, my hands were shaking so violently. This scared me, because as bad as migraine pain was, I understood it. I was familiar with it, and learned how to function with it when necessary. This new pain was well beyond that, and I was terrified.

Trying to dial the phone was equally frustrating, my fingers were shaking so bad. I mistyped the number more than once. After several attempts, I finally got through to Vicky. Tears were pouring down my face as I attempted to tell her what was happening. Good thing caller ID informed her who was calling, because I was a mess. When I did manage to get out some words, she immediately discerned something was wrong and shifted into high alert. Her questions quickly changed, trying to determine what was wrong.

Haphazardly, I was able to communicate the excruciating pain in my head. She said she would come get me as soon as she could. Fortunately, Vicky got ahold of a dear friend who was still up and able to bring her.

It took about forty-five minutes before she arrived, during which time I do not have a very good recollection of what happened. I remember my eyes were blurry and it was hard to do anything. I also know there are periods I can't remember whatsoever. For example, I remember being in pain when I hung up the phone, and the next moment I was in the bathroom, losing everything I'd ever thought of eating. How I got from my desk to the bathroom, I had no idea. I mean, I'm sure I walked, but I do not remember it.

Vicky called my cell phone and I answered it in the bathroom. She was outside, and I told her I would be out as soon as I could. I remember closing the phone and then… nothing.

For the next forty-five minutes.

She waited in the parking lot for a long time before a security guard finally drove over to ask why she was there (as this was a secure defense contractor facility). She informed him of the situation, explaining I was somewhere in the building, possibly in the bathroom, and in pain. He entered the building and began searching for me, finding me on the floor in a hallway near the exit.

"Is your name Patrick?" he asked.

"Yes," I said, trying to focus on him.

I had no idea how I got to the hallway, or how I'd gotten my bag, or how I wound up on the floor. The guard helped me to my feet and out to my car. I remember getting in the passenger side of the car, the door shutting and then everything went black.

The following is a recollection from Vicky about what happened from that point on Sunday through to Thursday:

With Pat in the car, I raced toward Texas Health HEB hospital. There were closer hospitals, but I didn't know how to get to them and didn't have time to figure it out. I determined the time would be better spent racing him to a hospital than looking at maps.

Along the way, Pat was flailing his arms around. At one point, he managed to knock the drive shift into neutral. I hadn't noticed this and instead thought the car had died on me. I was about to have a major panic as I didn't know why the car wasn't moving no matter how much I pushed on the gas.

In my distress, I managed to flag down a man who was running and asked him to help me. I don't know who he was, but he offered to go get his truck, put Pat in and race him to the hospital. I'd told him I felt there was no time for an ambulance.

It was at this moment when I noticed the car was in neutral. I quickly informed the man and took off, not getting the chance to thank him for being so willing to help me in a moment of need.

I pulled up to the Emergency Room (ER) entrance and jumped out, calling for help. A mixture of nurses and orderlies came to my aid, getting Patrick out of the car and onto a gurney. They told me to leave my car there and someone would move it later. We all raced into the ER and immediately into a vacant room.

Within seconds a large amount of people surrounded Patrick and began working on him. I stood there helpless, watching them do things I'd only seen on television programs. A nurse came and took me to a small waiting room. Seconds seemed like days as I waited to hear any news.

About fifteen minutes passed before a doctor finally came into the room. He explained Pat was in really bad shape, and that he wasn't going to make it through the night. If there was anyone I needed to call, now was the time.

At this point, I realized I had my cell phone on me, but not Pat's. His phone had everyone's numbers in it, while mine only had a very small handful. (We would later find out Pat had dropped his phone in the bathroom.) This didn't stop me from making some calls.

First was to an elder woman in our church who had been an ICU and ER nurse. I told her what was going on, and she said she would let the pastor and others know. Then I called my sister and my father-in-law, both of whom were shocked, supportive, and told me that they would look for the fastest way to make it from the northeastern US to Texas.

As I continued to wait for news on Pat, our Pastor and his wife arrived to sit and pray with me. They were troopers, getting the call at midnight and immediately heading down to the hospital to stay a good portion of the night with me.

After several hours they informed me they had to put Pat into an induced coma so they could stabilize him. Even though he wasn't expected to last the night, they were going to move him out of the ER into an Intensive Care Unit (ICU) room. They said the ICU had strict rules on visiting, even for close family, and I couldn't see him until seven in the morning.

SEVEN in the morning.

My husband was dying in some room in the hospital, and I wouldn't be allowed to see him until seven — unless they called me to inform me he had passed.

This didn't sit well with me, but I had children at home and decided going home and trying to sleep was a good idea. In addition, the doctor on staff told me there really wasn't anything more that I could do but go home, get some rest and come back in the morning.

After arriving at home, I informed Sam (the friend who drove me to Pat's work and returned home to watch the kids) what was going on. Katie woke up and asked me what was happening. I remember telling her about her Dad being in the hospital and that he needed prayer.

Obviously, I wasn't going to tell a thirteen-year-old that her Dad was possibly dying. Even if I wanted to, I'm not sure I would have had the words. After that, I attempted to get some sleep (as if anyone could really sleep under those conditions). Instead I spent a bunch of the night praying for my husband.

Monday morning came and I needed to get back to Pat and hear what the doctors were saying. However, I had three kids at home, ages 13, 11 and 4. I sent Abby to school while keeping Katie to watch James.

Arriving in the ICU, I found my husband surrounded by ten doctors. They told me it was a miracle he had lasted the night, but to not get my hopes up because they determined his kidneys had failed and there was currently no brain activity. The doctors attempted to bring him out of the induced coma, but he tossed about so violently the orderlies had a difficult time restraining him, so they put him back under.

The doctors informed me this wasn't a good sign, saying even if he did manage to wake up he would be a vegetable and need months and months of physical therapy just to do the fundamental things, like feeding himself. I looked at Pat, with all the tubes and machines attached to him, and began to pray. Whenever I was allowed in his room, I would place the Bible on his chest and pray.

At some point during Monday morning, the friend who had retired from being an ICU and ER nurse came into the room. She was a Godsend, explaining all the bags and IVs and machines and tubes that were connected to Pat. In addition, she told me to go ahead and sign the document for a PICC line. (They had asked me to do this earlier, but I didn't know what it was and it sounded horrible, having a direct line to his heart.) After her explanation and assurance it was a good thing, I allowed them to put one in, and it was a really good thing.

The remainder of the day had me going from my husband's side to home, handling the kids' needs. I was too exhausted to think about what could happen, but kept praying.

152

Tuesday morning rolled around and I was able to find someone to watch James, allowing the girls to go to school. I'd informed the school what was going on, and they told me that they would have counselors on hand to help them in case either needed them.

The doctors informed me they were going to try and take Pat out of the coma and basically let whatever was going to happen to him happen. They didn't have much hope, but I had my hope in God, and continued to pray. The first signs out of the coma seemed to confirm the doctor's fears that Pat couldn't feed himself or even be able to move around. He looked really, really out of it. When I looked in his eyes, it was as if he was no longer there. He was blinking and breathing and looking back at me, but no one was home.

No matter what I saw, I continued to pray and stand by his side, all while informing everyone via phone of the updates of his condition. Family out of state were still trying to gather the funds to make the trip and everything seemed bleak.

But God… God had a different plan.

Wednesday arrived, and I had the same plan with the kids as the day before. The doctors continued to be amazed my husband wasn't already dead, but also continued to assert his old life was gone and everything was going to be different and I should prepare myself, mentally and emotionally.

Pat looked better, although there was still a lot he couldn't do himself. At one point he wanted to leave, and I told him, "If you can get up out of that bed, you can leave!" Obviously, he wasn't able to do this, as he wasn't even able to lift himself up for the bedpan. But he did seem more alert.

Mick, our oldest and dearest friend, came to visit him, sit with me for a while and even helped feed Pat. I continued to pray and lay the Bible on Pat's chest because I knew I served a God who performed miracles every day.

Thursday I wasn't able to get up in the morning to hear from the doctors, as getting my girls off to school ate up more time than expected. In addition, finding someone to watch James took a lot longer than I would have liked. I was exhausted by all of this running around, not sleeping well and trying to be strong for everyone, all while praying with every ounce of my being for Pat to be healed.

However, when I managed to finally get the kids taken care of, I returned to the hospital and sat by Pat's side. On the way to the hospital I got the most amazing call, "Your husband is awake! I mean, he is <u>really</u> awake, and he's asking for you!"

I could barely drive, I was so happy.

I'm so thankful for the amazing woman God has blessed me with as my wife. I know these few days were insanely hard, but she managed to keep everyone in sync and informed, juggling the kids every minute of the day and spending a lot of time at my side and storming the gates of heaven. I am truly blessed!!

Thursday morning, September 27th at around 9:30a.m., I woke up. To be clear, when I say "I woke up," I'm saying I sat up by myself, just as if I'd been taking an extended nap since Sunday night. My eyes were wide open and alert, I was sitting up in the bed, and I was completely whole, fully myself again.

I remember opening my eyes and doing a quick assessment of my situation. I knew I was in a hospital, and I surmised I wasn't in a regular emergency room, but had been moved for observation to an ICU room, due to all the medical technology. Since I'm kind of a smart guy, I figured I'd been here for the night and it was most likely Monday morning. Little did I know what really happened.

I still remember the nurse coming in to check on my vitals and the shocked look on her face when I said, "Hello!" She almost leapt for joy at the sound of my voice, nearly dropping what she was carrying.

"Your wife is going to be so happy!!" she said, then explained how it was Thursday and I'd been in a coma for several days. I didn't believe her, to be honest, although I'm not sure why not. I mean, she had no reason to lie to me, but I just didn't believe her, as if my mind refused to accept what she was saying. She had to turn on the television and set it to the news before I would accept that it was, indeed, Thursday.

I was in shock, immediately worrying about how this had affected my family.

Before my wife would come back to the hospital, all nine of my doctors would come in and examine me. Each one was shocked, walking into the room and seeing me sitting up, awake and alert. Each one would do an assessment and tell me they were surprised to see me alive, much less sitting up, talking and being myself. Not really comprehending what happened, I responded to each of them the same way. "God healed me!"

All nine had the same response to my statement. "If that's what you want to believe," they would say, before turning and walking out.

If that's what I wanted to believe?!

These were the medical professionals, the ones who knew *exactly* the level of God's miracle they were looking at, and yet they all refused to acknowledge it. Later the doctor who was overseeing the case, along with the kidney and the heart doctor, would all use the word "miracle," but when I said God did, it they would back off and downplay it.

I cannot tell you how sweet the sound of Vicky's voice was when I heard her speaking to the nurse in the hallway before entering the room. The nurse simply said, "He's awake!" and my wife burst into the room, throwing back the curtain and practically sailing to the bed to get to me and give me a kiss.

I will never forget the look of intense love and relief I saw in her eyes, seeing me sitting up on my own and looking back into her eyes. She saw me and she *knew* I was back. For me it was like I went to sleep and woke up the next morning... only it was four days later. For her, it had been a constant battle and ordeal, one through which she stood firm against all the attacks of the enemy. She stood strong when I couldn't, empowered by God Himself as she beat the devil off of me.

Man, I love my wife.

She later recounted to me all that had happened. The doctors told me that eventually I would remember the missing time, but as of this writing (some fifteen years later) I still don't remember any more than I did when I first woke up.

After spending some time talking with me, hugging and kissing me, Vicky told me that I'd better never put her through an ordeal like that again. I promised her I wouldn't, and praise God that, with His help, I've been able to keep it.

The morning of Saturday September 29th, they moved me out of the ICU and into a regular hospital room. They told me to expect several months of recovery to get me back functioning and on my feet, since I'd been in such bad shape. God had a different plan, which included given me new kidneys.

The doctors had determined that a blood pressure drug, Tarka (which has since been pulled from the market because of causing kidney failure), combined with the high dose of ibuprofen (which in rare cases can cause kidney issues), essentially caused my kidneys to fail. This sent my body into a panic mode, as the kidneys filter your blood. When they shut down, your blood becomes toxic and starts causing other systems in your body to have issues, ultimately causing them to shut down. And when that happens, death soon follows.

In my case, it wasn't looking good for me, which is why they put me in an induced coma to attempt to stop the systematic shutdown and stall the process. By the time I got to the hospital, medically it was too late. Yet God stepped in and gave me a supernatural transplant of brand new kidneys.

No surgery. No worry about rejection or matching or anything else. God just gave me new ones, and I'm forever thankful.

On Tuesday, October 2, 2007, they released me from the hospital. They told me that outside of high blood pressure, they could find nothing medically wrong with me. Just a week prior they were telling my wife I would die, and there I was, walking out of the hospital. (Well, okay, I was wheeled out to the car and then was able to stand and walk, but I was released because I was more than fine.)

My kidneys were operating better than normal. The rest of my systems were all back to working fine. Everything was good, and there was no reason to keep me in the hospital.

After I was released, I visited my primary care doctor as instructed by the hospital for a follow up. He's now a friend of mine and a fellow believer. He told me the hospital called him back when I was admitted and told him, "We have one of your patients and he's not going to make it through the night!" He told me he immediately started praying for me. He was *exceptionally* excited to see me walking into his office.

This is an immense stone in my altar, because I should have died. Instead God healed me, and I'm forever thankful. Since then, I've had a ton of great memories with my family and I've been able to see my kids grow and go to college and become young adults. I've been able to be there when Katie became engaged to the love of her life (and an all-around great guy). I'll be able to be there for her, to walk her down the aisle and give her away.

I will be there when my other daughter gets married, when my son meets and marries the love of his life. For all the amazing things that have been and are coming, I am forever thankful to God for healing me and saving my life.

MAILBOX MIRACLE

'Heal me, O Lord, and I will be healed;
Save me and I will be saved, For You are my praise.'
- Jeremiah 17:14

In 2007, God gave me new kidneys (see He Shall Not Die), but I wasn't out of the woods yet. When the hospital released me, they handed me twelve prescriptions. *12!*

To be fair, I think I was on three prior to the hospital visit. Still, there were a lot of new ones, and I fulfilled all of them. Why? Because I'd been "mostly dead" (for all you Princess Bride fans) for several days, and I wasn't about to argue with my wife over the prescriptions. I saw the toll the stay at the hospital had put her through, and the last thing I wanted was to add to that ordeal. So I fulfilled and took them all, as prescribed.

Almost immediately upon returning home, however, I started to have some additional health concerns. I began having blackout periods where I would lose anywhere from about a minute to an hour. Many times it was fairly harmless, like watching a movie and suddenly the credits are rolling or filling a pitcher of water to suddenly having it overflowing onto the floor.

Some weren't so harmless, however, like the time I was sitting in the passenger seat of a car and suddenly arrived home. Times like that, I was thankful my wife and I knew better than to have me driving. All of them were kind of super scary, to be honest.

I also began experiencing what I called seizures. My body would start to shake, and I had no control over it. It would start in my hands or feet, rapidly taking over my whole body for about five to ten minutes at a time, typically happening about a dozen times a day.

This freaked me out. To look at a part of your body doing something you didn't tell it to do — and then not stopping as you were telling it to — was beyond terrifying. Sometimes I shouted out loud for it to stop. It didn't. It was so otherworldly, like I was looking at someone else's body, since I should have control over my own.

They were way too frequent and way too long to be anything *but* worrisome. Finally, I was having trouble concentrating. I'd originally attributed this to the blackouts and seizures, but as things progressed day to day and week to week, it was obviously something more. At one point I returned to work (against doctor's orders) and wasn't able to do my job. I just couldn't summon the cognitive power to do what used to be easy for me. Of all the issues I was facing, this was the most terrifying. The *last* thing I wanted was to become disabled and unable to provide for my family. Thankfully God had a plan… I just didn't know it yet.

Vicky knew. Wives know these things. If you're a wife, you know what I'm talking about. I think it's a God-given gift that a wife knows what's happening with her husband, even when nothing specific is said. When she would see me and ask how I was, I would blow her off. Not because I wasn't feeling the problem, but because I didn't want to put her through another ordeal. (Note: you can think you're hiding something from your spouse, but chances are they already know.)

Eventually, I told her what I was feeling. Immediately she started praying over me for healing and continued to do so until this was gone. She was an amazing rock who always knew that whatever this was, I was going to be healed from it. I wasn't nearly as confident, but then I'd just slept through the super huge miracle she'd walked through. This didn't stop me from questioning and being concerned.

I kept asking God, "Why would you spare my life if I'm only going to be living with these debilitating problems?" I was confused and very frustrated. It didn't make any sense, and being an engineer — a person of intense logic — this confounded me. *Especially* since I couldn't find any pattern to when these attacks would occur.

It didn't matter what I'd been doing or not doing. It didn't matter what I'd eaten or not eaten, if I drank enough fluids or not. Nothing seemed to precede the random times the attacks would come. I began to wonder how I could declare the wondrous healing power of God, when I was walking around blacking out and shaking all over the place.

It didn't connect, and it really felt like I could never share or call what had happened a miracle. Kind of like a severely overweight person trying to tell someone else how to be thin. Or imagine I was preaching some Sunday about God and His miraculous healing power, giving my testimony and then, just as I round into my third point, I black out. Or begin to shake all over… or have an altar call and start praying over people but then can't remember how to pray or what to pray for.

Who would believe my testimony? I began to feel like a fake, even though I had legitimately been saved from death. Worse, I began to blame God for my current issues, which was exactly where the devil wanted me to be.

Of course, these were the wrong questions and thoughts. God wasn't doing this to me. He wasn't responsible for my issues, and He certainly didn't save my life only to debilitate it. In fact, with what I know today, I can confidently say God didn't want me to walk through *any* of this. But I'd been so blinded by the trauma I caused my family (and my own selfish pride), I was unable to hear what God was saying to me.

When I prayed, I brought a laundry list of things I felt God needed to fix. I didn't come to hear Him and I didn't come to have a conversation. Instead I just complained and blamed Him for everything, almost demanding He changed things. However, through this entire time God was still moving. I'm reminded of the book of Daniel when the angel finally shows up after he had been fasting for twenty-one days.

From October 2007 until June of 2008, I'd gone from one doctor to the next, from one test to the next. They checked my heart, my kidneys, my brain, my lungs and everything else they could think to test. I had X-rays, EKGs, EEGs, CAT scans, MRIs, Stress Tests, Sleep tests, and a host of other tests. Every single test they ran came back with the same report: I was in good to great health. Nothing was found. No abnormality. Nothing wrong!

Everything pointed to my being fine when things were anything, but this made me all the more frustrated because I knew that I knew something was wrong, but every test they ran couldn't find it. Because of the sheer volume of tests, I began to joke about how comic books were lying to us. I had radiation of one sort or another bombarded on me, smeared on me, injected into me and ingested, and I didn't develop a single superpower. Not one!

Humor was the only way I felt I could keep my sanity throughout this time period. At one point, I was actually praying the next test would find something — *anything* — just so I knew what was going on with my body. They could have told me at one point I had cancer, and I would have been happy knowing what the problem was. (But thank God I did not and do not have cancer.)

To make matters worse, this entire time I had to fight with the disability insurance company. Fortunately, my work had placed me on short-term disability, and then later long-term, which would mean I would get a paycheck while I was out, hopefully recovering from whatever had happened.

Since I wasn't actually diagnosed with a problem, however, the disability insurance company didn't know how to categorize me. What's worse, without a category they couldn't approve the claim, and when a claim is not approved they don't send checks. This meant week after week would pass *without any pay*. I believe I went a period of almost six weeks without a paycheck, returned to work briefly and then another period of about six months before this was figured out. Still, even in all this, God was faithful to us.

At one point, with no money coming in and bills piling up, I decided to return to work (against doctor's orders) just to get a paycheck again. I still remember walking back into work that first day, armed with a note from my doctor declaring I needed to be on light duty and working no more than forty hours a week. My boss looked at me and frowned. "We are way behind," he said. "If you want to keep your job, we need you to work *at least* sixty hours a week!"

What choice did I have? I was in desperate need of money and the overtime pay would certainly help. However, the return to work and the strain of working all that overtime — which ended up being more like 70-80 hours — only made my symptoms worse. I was blacking out more often, seizing several times an hour and tried to cope with the extreme ordeal of focusing on *anything* related to work. It got so bad I simply couldn't function, and had to be pulled out of work a second time.

The rounds with the doctors began again, including a new round of the same tests. Because we had crossed over into 2008, our insurance would pay for some of the tests to be rerun. Once again, I didn't have an official diagnosis for my condition and the disability insurance I'd paid for flat-out refused to pay me. I remember being on the phone with the account representative. "Let me get this straight," I asked, exasperated. "You're questioning my medically board-certified doctor's opinion that I'm unable to work?"

They'd reply they would be happy to pay me… if they could just get a diagnosis. I was fuming mad, and at one point lost my spirituality with them. "Tell you what," I growled. "If you could fax me your medical diploma so I know you have the right to question my doctor, then I will drop my claim!" Obviously, that didn't happen (and was the wrong attitude to have), but I was nearing my wit's end.

I didn't know what else to do. I couldn't get a diagnosis. Month after month, no money came in. It was a horribly frustrating, and I felt like I was simultaneously fighting an invisible enemy on two sides, one inside and one outside.

Today I can say that no matter how little money I got from work or how long I was out, God always took care of us. Sometimes it was someone bringing food, other times it was someone bringing money. One time a friend felt the need to basically send me my rent check because God laid my name on his heart. Another time we went to the food shelf and the lady felt so strongly for us she gave us a double portion. Time after time, act after gracious act, God took care of us through so many different people. This was truly a miracle.

Even with all God was doing, the financial strain was still hard on us, and probably did nothing for my health. It all came to a head on one Friday morning, when we woke up to discover an intent to evict notice on our door, declaring we had until close of business day to pay our rent or be kicked out. I must have read that note a dozen times, hoping against hope the words would change.

I was terrified. We had no money to go anywhere if they kicked us out, no options to come up with enough money to stay, let alone have it by end of the day! While I knew it would take another two weeks or so to actually evict us, we simply had no other place to go.

I laid in my bed praying. Shortly after noon, I rose from my bed, the weight of the world on my shoulders. I felt like such a failure to my family, and didn't want to look any of them in the eye. I would later learn that feeling of failure was all on me, as my family saw me as a husband, father, leader and constant source of great faith. I thank God for my family.

You might be asking, "What about your church family?" Normally, they would be rallying around us and praying with us. They would be maybe bringing over food and dropping little bits of money here and there, in benevolence for us. At least, that's what the church *should* be doing. Instead, the church we were attending at the time distanced themselves from us. At one point they declared we had obviously sinned or walked out of the will of God, and kicked us out. Shortly after, I literally received a letter revoking our membership!

I'd never heard of anything like that before. In the middle of our need, even the church had abandoned us. However — and this is critically important — God never abandoned us. At the time it made me even madder. I remember telling God, "*I love you, but I've absolutely had it with your people and want nothing to do with them!*"

So that Friday I told God He had to come through. I was out of options. God was my last resort, and the only answer He had left was to come through. My initial thought was God would put it on someone's heart to come, knock on our door out of the blue and hand us some money. This certainly would have been a true miracle from God, as no one was associating with us since the break with the church.

My second thought was I would walk out into the living area and find a pile of money on the table, miraculously deposited by an angel or maybe Jesus Himself. It would have everything we needed *plus some*, because He is a God of abundance. I knew God could do either of those things and infinitely more if He wanted to. In fact, I'd seen so many miracles in my life to this point, there was no way for me to *not* believe in God and His ability to somehow step into reality and perform a miracle to take care of our situation. But truth be told, as the day was half over, it was becoming harder and harder to hold on to hope.

Around three o'clock in the afternoon, I decided to go out and check the mail. Obviously, I was hoping there would be a check. Perhaps the insurance company finally sent me some money, even though I knew everything was still up in the air. Or perhaps someone we used to know was moved by God to send us money and today was the day we would get the check. Or perhaps a family member who wasn't aware of our situation just felt the sudden and urgent need to send us money.

Whatever the method or the reason, I was going to see if there was a check. My brother, who was staying with us, was sitting at the kitchen table as I walked out from my bedroom and headed toward the front door. He asked me where I was going. I looked at him and said, "I'm going to get the check that's in the mailbox!" He looked at me like I was from Mars as I made my way out the door.

Now, I would really love to tell you, as a blood-bought, song-singing, Bible-believing, born again Christian whom God had miraculously provided with new kidneys and had seen the hand of God move (as well as heard the audible voice of God), I was a pillar of confidence in my God, strutting over to the mailbox to get the check I'd just declared was in there.

I wasn't.

As soon as the door closed, I began begging God that there be some money — any money — in the mailbox so I could keep my family from being evicted. As I rounded the corner and walked past our patio's sliding glass doors, I straightened up and walked with the confidence I should have had, just in case my brother was looking. I didn't dare look over, for fear that if he were looking he might see I wasn't the anchor everyone — including him and his family — depended on. Instead, I kept my eyes straightforward and my gaze locked on our car in the parking lot in front of me.

A few moments of Pat the Pillar exuding confidence and grace, and I was past where my brother could see me, back to begging there would be a check in the mailbox. I remember saying to God, "You know if there isn't a check, it's going to reflect badly on you, as my brother is now expecting to see a miracle!" As if God was worried about His reputation with my brother or anyone else, for that matter. Suffice it to say, when you're desperate you're not exactly thinking straight.

I arrived at the mailbox and said one last prayer. I turned the key and opened the tiny door. There was a bunch of mail, which wasn't a surprise because we had a lot of bill collectors after us by this point. I closed and locked the mailbox, thumbing through what was there. I almost dropped the mail as shock suddenly raced through my body, stopping on one particular piece.

It was from the State of Texas, and it looked like a check. I quickly opened the envelope to discover a check for a whopping $2,100.

$2,100! More than enough to cover what we needed for rent *plus food*. I stood there in total and absolute shock. I don't think I moved for at least five minutes. If there had been a breeze, I would have fallen over, I was so astounded.

I thanked God profusely on my way back to the apartment. The reason there was a check was because this was the year President George W. Bush had issued tax refunds to all Americans to help with the recession. In that moment I didn't care where the check came from, just that God had sent one. (And through the government, no less!)

I remember standing outside the door to the apartment, puffing out my chest, standing straight and tall, taking a couple deep breaths and making sure to center myself as the same pillar I walked out acting like. I couldn't look shocked or surprised, or everyone would know I was just as much a wreck as they were. I had to maintain a stoic, firm stance on God, so they knew they, too, could count on Him.

I identified with Moses when the Israelites were backed up to the Red Sea. He had to be their anchor or else there would be a panic, because in the natural there was no way out. Soon they would all die, and there wasn't anything Moses could do about it except pray as he stared at the water and told everyone that God would find a way. I imagined the feeling I experienced at the mailbox was what Moses must have felt as he watched the waters go from being still to pulling back and revealing a dry path through to the other side.

Relief and excitement and awe and joy all in one moment, a moment you couldn't really enjoy because you had to go back to being the leader and affirm everyone else's faith was well-placed, because right here in front of them was the miracle we had been praying for.

I opened the door and entered the apartment. My brother was still sitting at the table as I strolled in. "So was there a check?" he inquired. There might have been some sarcasm or doubt in his tone, but his face turned pale when I produced the check from the state.

My wife had a huge smile. She grabbed her purse and headed immediately for the door, well aware we had to boogie to make it to the bank and back to the apartment office before they closed. God was good to us and we had favor with the bank manager who approved cashing the check for us so the entire amount was immediately available. We arrived at apartment business office moments before they closed, money order in hand to pay rent. It was all seemingly at the last moment to us, but obviously well within God's time. He shined through for us, and I'm super thankful.

Now to fully understand this miracle, you need to know the *rest* of the story.

One week later we got a letter from the state, informing us they would be mailing our refund check within a week, and we should expect to receive it within about two weeks after that. Only… we already *had* the check. But that wasn't the biggest part of the check miracle.

Vicky noticed the check was dated *for the Friday we received it* in the mail. In other words, they printed the check in Austin, had the United States Postal Service stamp it as regular mail (or maybe bulk) with the stamp date of that Friday and delivered it to our mailbox in the Dallas-Fort Worth area — *all on the same day*. There is simply no way a check coming from two hundred miles away could have been issued the same day we received it in the mail. But this is the kind of thing that can happen when God performs miracles.

This is a huge stone in my altar because it showed me how, no matter what you're walking through, God will never leave your side. We had no money and no natural hope, but God came through and continued to come through. Day after day, He showed up and helped us. We didn't always know how He was going to show up, but He always showed up. This allows me to walk through whatever may lay ahead, knowing in my heart God will always come through.

HOW DID YOU GET MY RESUMÉ?

'Behold, I will do something new, Now it will spring forth;
Will you not be aware of it? I will even make a roadway
in the wilderness, Rivers in the desert.'
- Isaiah 43:19

On Monday, January 9th, 2012, after seven years, I was let go from the defense firm I'd been working for. Initially, I was surprised, although I probably shouldn't have been. I'd missed a bunch of work because of my major health issues, and when coupled with a really bad attitude it kind of created a perfect recipe of being fired.

I also had a delusional idea God would just have to keep blessing me with the job, because I was giving and attending church. Only... I wasn't attending church, since we had left the one we were at beforehand. So we had no spiritual covering and a bad outlook, along with a horrible work ethic, and yet somehow I thought God simply wouldn't allow me to lose my job.

I felt betrayed as I walked out of the building to my car. Betrayed and... oddly elated.

What I didn't realize was the stress of the job was having a hugely negative impact on my health. My blood pressure was through the roof, and my doctor was having trouble finding a medicine to control it. I was having stomach issues. Headaches. The list went on.

Meanwhile, I was working long hours and often out of town. Over a two-year period, I was traveling for work around seventy-five percent of the time, working eighty plus hours a week. Even when I was home, the hours were the same (if not more). I don't think I was ever on a project that wasn't at least six months behind.

In fact, I remember one time our team was assigned a new project at nine in the morning, then attended a status meeting that same day at eleven to explain ourselves why we were six months behind deadline. We hadn't even had a chance to write a single line of code yet! But that's how this company worked, day in and day out, and all of that took a toll on me. Starting with my family life, followed by my health and finally my attitude. Leaving the company was one of the best feelings in my life. Well, until about halfway home when I realized I'd have to explain to my amazing wife I'd lost my job... again.

Finding myself searching back in a job market after seven years feels like a fish out of water. To further complicate things, this time around online resumé submissions really began to take off, allowing for employers to point potential applicants to a website to apply. In the old days you could go into a company and speak to someone in the Human Resources department and, if they were hiring, often speak directly to the hiring manager right then. Your chances increased dramatically if they had advertised they were hiring.

All that went out the window to the impersonal website submission. Now you sat at a computer and filled out websites and uploaded resumés and prayed for a call back. Today as I write this, the process has become super sophisticated by adding bots (computer software that acts like tiny robots) which sift through submissions for specific keywords or phrases or experience or whatever, and either push your resume forward or reject it immediately. All without you knowing.

Now, I wouldn't say I was very great at getting a job, but usually once I spoke with someone face-to-face I had a good chance. With this new way of submitting resumés, you could submit way more job applications in a day but almost no human contact, making the whole experience feel somewhat empty. *Especially* if you didn't get any call backs. All I could think about on the way home was how I was dreading having to search for a job. Again. Well, that, and how I was going to explain to my wife about the loss.

This was long before I subscribed to the philosophy that being honest was always the best approach. Instead, I felt like I had to put a positive spin on everything, so even though I didn't come out smelling like a rose, I also didn't stink like the dung heap I felt I was. I walked into the house and didn't need to say a word. I didn't have to. She already knew.

Of course, I still had to say the words. In this case, the specific words I'd rehearsed on the way home. I explained how it wasn't my fault, but those dirty rotten people at the company. I selfishly told her how cruel it was to let someone go just a couple of weeks before their birthday, let alone our 21st anniversary (my birthday is the 4th of February and our anniversary is the 9th, just five days later). I laid it on pretty thick, putting my best foot forward, and Vicky took it all in stride.

She didn't argue. She didn't get upset. She didn't get mad. She admitted she was disappointed, but stated it calmly, a more a matter of fact item than making me even more concerned. The only thing she did during this whole time was support me. I still don't know how she didn't take my head off in this moment, because I sure deserved it.

Before I share what happened next, it's important to note that when I started working for the defense company, I deactivated any accounts on job search sites. My father had always informed me to work at a company a minimum of two years before you look to move to another. So without actively looking, I didn't get calls or emails, which meant my profile was virtually nonexistent, and all copies of my resumé had been removed.

A couple of days after losing my job, I was still updating my resumé, searching for just the right way to say what I did at the previous job so it passed the bots. I looked online at examples and did my best to ensure I crafted everything with the most keywords to get my resumé to the top of the virtual stacks. It was at this time I received a very strange call from a software recruiter for a technology contract firm.

The man mentioned he worked with an airline company to help them acquire talent, but the reason it was strange was he stated he was looking at my resumé... while we were on the phone. The position they had opened was for a short-term software developer with a small chance of being hired on as a regular employee. (He was quick to point out that this wasn't a guarantee, but a potential opportunity.)

Obviously, God was opening a door for me, yet I sat there all befuddled. He had a few questions for me based on my resumé and this is where it got really, *really* weird for me. Why? Because most of the questions centered around my previous employer. I remember I asked him multiple times, "You're looking at my resumé?" To which he would reply, "Yes." I imagine I must have sounded like Mr. Banks from the classic movie Mary Poppins, in the scene when she's reading to him a letter he knew he tore up and threw in the fireplace.

Allow me to explain a bit further why I was so befuddled. The recruiter's questions made it obvious he wasn't looking at an older version of my resumé, nor was he looking at any copy of my resumé which existed *anywhere on the internet*. Instead, he was looking at a version that only existed in the present, on my home computer. The resumé I was still editing.

I was still working on it and hadn't come to a place where I felt it was ready to publish. This would mean unless this firm hacked in my computer, found where I stored my current resumé and downloaded a copy, there was no way for them to have a copy. To drive this point even further home, he was quoting from edits I'd made to the resumé only the night before.

Following the phone interview I checked literally everywhere on the internet to see if I could find any copy of my resumé that had anything about my recent job. I found nothing. I didn't have a LinkedIn account, hadn't shared anything on Facebook. None of the job search sites had a copy of my active or updated resumé, and the ones that were deactivated were all old and outdated. There simply was no explainable way this recruiter could have had a copy of the resumé that sat on my computer, unless God had given it to him.

The face-to-face interview with the airline company took place a week later. I arrived early with copies of my resumé, cover letter, and references. I met the recruiter in the Human Resource lobby and we chatted for about fifteen minutes. During this time, I asked him to take a look at the copy of my resumé he had so I could make sure he had the most recent.

Sure enough, it was identical to the ones I brought with me, the ones which still only existed on my home computer. On the phone the recruiter said I was a perfect fit for this job, however looking at the job requisite I felt I wasn't. I didn't have most of the recommended skills and met very few of the requirements. However, I was already there and hadn't anything to lose by doing the interview. I said a quick prayer before being taken back.

The interview with the hiring manager was... also strange. He didn't ask me any questions, save for one at the very end. Instead he talked airlines. He talked about the project. He talked about how he was living two states to the north and flew down every week to work. He would leave on Monday morning to come directly there, work until late on Thursday and then fly back home. The company had been agreeable to his schedule and even helped with his flights (because, after all, they *were* an airline).

At the end, after reminiscing about his work week schedule, he turned to me, looked me in the eye and asked, "Can you do the job?"

Even though I was surprised by this bizarro interview, I quickly replied, "Yes!"

He then thanked me and walked out.

I had no idea if I did good or bad, if I would get a job offer or not. I walked out confused and more than a bit dazed as I met back up with the recruiter. He asked me how it went, and I told him I wasn't sure because the manager did all the talking. The recruiter told me that was a good sign with this manager and they should know by the end of the week. Two days later I got the offer to come work there as a contractor.

I was still in shock at how this whole thing went down, but in a good way. Because of how quickly I got this job and the large pay rate, our finances only experienced a very small hit. God technically saved my butt by getting me a new job, and one that would give me additional training and new skills I would need to get the *next* job He gave me.

This is a humongous stone in my altar because it showed me there is no obstacle that's too big or too tall or too wide that God can't level and make a way for you. That version of my resumé never saw the internet because by the time I revisited it, I'd changed it to include this position. Yet, the recruiter had a copy he claimed he found on the internet.

The only way was that God put it in front of his eyes. I wasn't a perfect fit for the job but the recruiter said I was. The only way was God showed him something I never saw. The interview was bizarre, and there wasn't anything in it to indicate I should get the job — especially since there were other candidates. The only way I was employed that week was God whispering to the hiring manager I was the one before he even entered the room (which would explain why he didn't have any questions). In every aspect of this job, the only way to it was God, and I'm super thankful He loves me and blesses me, even when I do not remotely deserve it.

AN UNEXPECTED VISIT

*'And he carried me away in the Spirit
to a great and high mountain, and showed me the holy city,
Jerusalem, coming down out of heaven from God,'*
- Revelation 21:10

On May 4th, 2014, my father passed away. He had been battling with heart issues and I knew any time I saw or spoke with him could be the last. However, this didn't prepare me for the moment I got the call.

I remember vividly my father's friend calling on the phone in tears. I remember going into crisis mode and talking with the hospital, the police, the fireman, the EMT, the Careflight staff, identifying the body, working with the funeral home and on and on.

God was good in that we had a great relationship. By the time he had passed, he had become my best friend (next to my wife). We spoke for hours and hours at a time, and I looked forward to every moment we spent together. This is probably why his death hurt so much. By the grace of God, I managed to get through all of that while leaning on my family.

One of the questions I had for God about my father was whether he changed his permanent residence to heaven, or was he not to be counted among the saints? I know my Dad believed in God and in Jesus, and at one time was very much into going to a Bible church, reading his Bible and praising God. But somewhere along the way he lost the appeal of meeting with God's people and stopped going to church. Sometime after that, he would start talking about universalism, believing all religions point to the same single God.

He would expound upon how the God he knew wouldn't be so picky or closed to just one path, but allow all paths that even remotely resembled some of his form go to him. He would still be quick to say his chosen religion was Christianity, but the rest of his talk often was contradictory to the Bible, and even contradictory in itself. Many religions, especially when compared to Christianity, are at odds with each other, making it impossible to be worshipping the same God. So I had doubts he was now walking streets of gold.

I began asking God for a sign — any sign — that would tell me my Dad was in heaven. I wasn't picky, either. I just wanted something that would convince me beyond a shadow of a doubt. I'd assumed God would send me a very specific style of rainbow that was set apart, maybe seen in multiples. The reason I thought this was, when my mother had passed away, my Dad asked for a sign she was happy and no longer in pain. God brought my Dad to a mountain in the Adirondacks and showed him seven rainbows in the sky at once, without a cloud in the sky. He knew this was the sign from God my Mom was in heaven, happy and healthy. So I'd thought God would do something similar for me, and I kept my eyes on the skies.

June 15, 2014, started out like any other Father's Day Sunday. I'd gotten up and dressed and was off to church, shortly after arriving and taking seats in the back and proceeded to worship. I would sit in the back because with the meds I took I would often need to use the bathroom and didn't want to disturb others. I remember being a bit down, because I hadn't yet seen a sign about my Dad. While there was no specific time limit on God, I'd assumed he would answer my prayer rather quickly, but there I was a month later and hadn't seen anything. I was more than a bit disappointed.

The worship was good, but I found no matter how hard I tried I couldn't get into the spirit or the mood. Eventually, I sat down, closed my eyes and prayed, almost in tears.

Suddenly the music stopped and I heard birds chirping. It reminded me of waking up in my grandparents' house with the windows cracked in the summer in New Jersey. A warm breeze would fill the room as the melodic sounds of birds filled the air, and ever since then I loved the sound of birds singing. It's a very fond, warming and precious memory, a moment when I'm surrounded by an overwhelming feeling of love and peace.

I opened my eyes and froze. I could barely believe what I was seeing. I was no longer in the church! Instead, I stood in the foyer of medium-sized home, staring at the front door made of stained glass depicting the image of the sun and its rays. The walls were hard to explain, as they were painted a golden, sunbathed yellow. They were super vibrant and seemed to be glowing or at least emitting their own light. All of the colors seemed to be extremely vivid and glowing — emanating their own light without any visible power source or lamps.

Today I know this was coming from God, but in the moment I just stood in amazement. White trim ran around the baseboards as well as the ceiling, outlining the golden yellow walls. Everywhere I looked, the colors were bright and emanating light, but not so much it hurt my eyes. Quite the contrary, in fact. My eyes seemed at ease, not straining to see, even though I didn't have my glasses on. It was the most amazing thing I had ever seen.

I began to move backwards from the foyer toward my right, entering a living room. There were a lot of windows with very light, lacey white curtains painted with yellow birds, blowing gently in the breeze. I couldn't see outside the window, as it was a lot brighter than the room. At the center of the wall on my right was a large fireplace with an ornate white mantle and columns in an almost Romanesque style. Above the fireplace was a mirror, in which I could see a reflection of the room.

In the middle of the room were two couches facing each other, both with floral patterns on a creamy white base. There was a coffee table in the middle of the room as well, as a few end tables and a small sitting area near the windows. The furniture looked very Victorian, and I immediately thought, "This is exactly the kind of furniture my mother would have loved!" The walls were the same as the foyer, glowing golden yellow trimmed in white. There was a throw rug in the center of the room, but otherwise the floors were a brightly-colored, stained wood.

As I continued to move backwards, I spun around at the end of the living room to face the back of the house, staring at a dining room. The dining room table was rustic, with eight spindle backed chairs placed around it. The back wall was floor-to-ceiling window panels, also so bright with the exterior light I couldn't see outside. The brilliance of the outside light should have been causing me pain, but it actually felt good and warm. I would have stared at those windows for a really long time if the sound of a woman gasping hadn't drawn my attention to my right.

I looked over and there, seated at the head of the table, was my father. Behind him in a very large, dark cherry stained, rustic country style kitchen with a huge island stood my mother, making pancakes. Recognizing me standing there at their table, both of my parents smiled the biggest grins I'd ever seen them smile. They were almost too big, as if they knew something I didn't, which was an odd feeling as they were living in heaven and obviously knew a lot more than I did. I watched my mother walk over and stand next to my father.

Thumping sounds radiated from the ceiling above my father, drawing my attention. I instinctively looked up. I'd first thought maybe it was thunder, but it was too short and in too quick of rapid succession that I quickly dismissed it. The thumping traveled across the ceiling and then down a staircase I hadn't noticed in the foyer. The thumping soon changed to the familiar sounds of bare feet on wood, and a second later two small children burst into the open dining area. A boy and a girl raced over to sit on the opposite side of the table from where I stood.

The girl was maybe nine years old with beautiful, golden blonde hair. She was wearing a simple white blouse and white shorts, similar to what one would wear to the beach. She had striking blue eyes that drew me in, and soft facial features. She looked amazingly familiar, looking to my Dad and then back at me, grinning.

Somehow I knew she didn't have a name. I wish I could tell you how I knew this piece of information, but I can't. I just knew. What's more, I understood this fact also made her sad, which made me sad. I looked at her and felt a strange connection I couldn't understand or truly explain. It was almost as if I had become empathically linked to her.

The boy looked approximately five years old, with platinum blonde hair that looked just slightly better than if he had just rolled out of bed. His hair was disheveled and his clothes looked like they could have been slept in. He was wearing a white shirt with yellow short sleeves and the same style white shorts as the girl. He sat next to her and had deep brown eyes. He also looked familiar to me, and I felt I was connected to him just like I was the girl. I also knew his name was Joshua — Joshua Glen, to be specific.

My Dad cleared his throat drawing my attention and said, "I got this." He was shaking his head slightly up and down in affirmation. "You have done so much for me, I got this for you!" As if I suddenly received a massive download of information, I instantly knew exactly what he had meant. I suddenly knew both of these children were the ones Vicky and I had lost due to miscarriages.

I knew God had taken them to heaven, where they seemed to be growing up. I knew my Dad was telling me he was sent there by God to help raise his grandkids — my babies. I also knew God had granted him the chance of taking great care of them as a gift to me, because of all I'd done for my mother and father.

I couldn't hold back the tears as all of this information hit me like a flood. Honestly, if I'd been here in my normal body on a normal day and this much information had been poured into my mind, I would be overloaded. But there in heaven, it was absolutely glorious.

Immediately my parent's house in heaven disappeared and everything was black. I was back in the church as worship was still going on.

Honestly, I was in shock, tears running down my face. I couldn't believe what I'd just seen and experienced. I certainly couldn't explain it to anyone. Honestly, even as this retelling pales to capture the intensity of how great heaven truly was. I just sat there in that single seat next to my wife the whole rest of the service. I've no idea what was preached. I've no idea what I must have looked like because people tended to steer clear of me.

Later at lunch with Vicky and Katie, I shared with them what I'd seen, emotions flooded the dining area of the McDonald's as all of us started crying. Especially when I got to the part of our children who were living in heaven with my parents.

Later that night, I sat down with Vicky. I'd left out the part about the girl not having a name because I was already exhausted from what I'd shared, and I wasn't sure I could handle it at lunch. But when we were alone, I told her about the girl. When we lost her we didn't know what the sex was, and didn't know what name to use.

The boy we lost knowing he was a boy, and had the name Joshua Glen already picked out. Later when James would come along, we knew we couldn't reuse that name, although at the time we didn't know why. Today I know it was because it was taken. But the little girl we never named.

I looked at Vicky and said, "We have to give her a name!" Tears running down both of our faces, she agreed with me. It took us literally seconds to know what to name her. This was kind of amazing, because it took us weeks and months to come up with the other children's names. But this little girl's name we knew instantly.

We grabbed each other's hands and prayed to God, "Tell our little girl her name is Isabella Hope!" I know that I know that I know that God gave my little girl her name that night, and I can't thank or praise God enough.

This is one of the largest stones in my altar because I simply can't express how much this meant to me. To see the children we lost. To know my parents are well and in heaven. To be able to tell our daughter her name.

No words could ever do justice in describing how much this has impacted me, nor could they explain how much I long for the day we'll be reunited with our children.

SUNDAY'S COMING

*'Yet, with respect to the promise of God, he didn't waver in unbelief
but grew strong in faith, giving glory to God, and being fully assured
that what God had promised, He was able also to perform.'*
- Romans 4:20-21

My grandmother bought us a house back in 2011, which was an amazing testimony of love and God's provision. However, owning a mortgage-free home is a huge task, especially if you're under a mountain of pre-existing debt and were never that good at managing your money. This is exactly where Vicky and I found ourselves as we rapidly approached 2017.

We reached out to our church and the elders came to us with two recommendations. First, cut everything to the bone and adhere to a super-strict budget, then after about seven years we would begin to see some light at the end of the debt tunnel. I'm not exaggerating on the length of time. It was going to take a long, long time before we would have enough extra money in a month to afford even one of us eating at McDonald's. If we went with this plan, they told us we would have to pray hard that we didn't incur any extra expenses, like the pool pump or HVAC breaking down, because we would have literally no extra money to afford any repairs.

The second option was to sell the house, take the money and get completely out of debt. They determined if we got a little over two hundred thousand for the house we could get completely out of debt, possibly with ten to twenty thousand left to put in the bank. As much as we *loved* living in a house over an apartment, the choice was clear and we opted to sell the house.

I never realized how much work selling a house would take. Our pastor was a realtor and his wife was an interior decorator. They instructed us on exactly how to stage our home to sell. First, we had to paint every room a neutral color, a trail dust beige. Second, we had to minimize the furniture, moving some of it to the garage to make the house look spacious (even though it was a four bedroom with twenty-six hundred square feet). Third, we had to have all the rugs and floors professionally cleaned.

Fourth, we had to clean literally every surface as clean as possible. Fifth, we had to make the outside look amazing. (Curb appeal is everything). Sixth, we had to remove anything that was personal to us. Prospective buyers want to envision *themselves* in the house, and not pictures of you and your family. Finally, whenever there was a showing we had to make sure all the beds were made, we vacuumed all the floors, all the Scentsy potpourris were on and, if possible, bake some cookies so the fresh-baked smell permeated the home.

Our realtor told us a few hundred to a thousand dollars in paint and cleaning supplies could add ten to twenty thousand to the offer price. We were super motivated, and did everything they asked of us. After a few viewings we closed, selling the house on May 9th, 2017.

This meant we needed a new place to live, and soon we found a four bedroom rental. The place was fantastic and spacious for an apartment, having almost two thousand square feet. In addition to this, it was in the next town over which, as it turned out, would send James to a different school district for his high school years. This meant all the bullies who had messed with him would no longer be around. Honestly, this alone was enough to get us to sell and move. So we returned to apartment life and were thankful for how God continued to bless us and provide for us.

The apartment was great... for a time.

Everything was great... for a time.

However, eventually this feeling waned and we wanted to own a house again, for a variety of reasons.

First, it's so much nicer to be building equity than just paying rent. Second, we missed being able to put Christmas decorations up outside the house. But the biggest reason we wanted to get a home was for our two dogs. Daisy is a Great Pyrenees, Great Wolf Hound and Collie mix which is a rather large dog. On her hind legs she can stand over four feet tall. Kira is an Alaskan Malamute and Husky mix which is also a large dog. She is slightly longer and much thicker than Daisy.

These amazing furry babies were super about living with us in the apartment, but needed some space to be able to stretch their legs. They needed a backyard they could run around in. (Especially Daisy). So we went to the Lord in prayer, and between Thanksgiving and Christmas 2021, He confirmed He was going to get us a house. We couldn't have been more excited as we rounded the New Year.

Our original plan was to wait for an April-May timeframe to get a mortgage, because we had been working on our credit score and had determined it would be around then before it was good enough. However, toward the end of January 2022 our scores suddenly popped up into the mid 600s, and both Vicky and I felt like the moment had come. We immediately delved into Zillow and began looking at houses in the local area around our estimated budget. There were quite a few choices. We saved a few homes and began praying about next steps.

When my grandmother had bought us the previous house, we quickly learned the importance of making a housing list of absolute needs versus wants. We needed a backyard with ample space for the dogs. We needed a ranch-style, single-story home for the sake of our knees. We needed four bedrooms, as Vicky and I both worked from home and needed the space for an office. We needed a kitchen that wasn't a hallway. We needed a master bathroom.

One of the first things on the wants, or the gosh-it-sure-would-be-nice-to-have list, was a large kitchen. We wanted a double oven. We wanted a pool. We wanted a well laid out floor plan and at least two thousand square feet. We wanted a covered patio of some kind. We wanted a garage, or at least parking on the property (and yes, some houses do not have a driveway or places to park except on the street).

When my grandmother bought the previous house, God had provided us everything on *both* lists. We didn't know if He was going to do the same thing now, but knew if we didn't make these lists it would be harder to know if a house was a good fit later.

After I saved my first house in Zillow, a representative called me the following day. I almost didn't answer the call, as I didn't recognize the number but fortunately the Caller ID said it was Zillow. They had seen my activity and were reaching out to see if there was anything they could do to help. This was both unexpected and super nice of them. I told them we had just started and didn't yet know what we would need. Then the representative asked, "Are you working with a realtor?"

The one we worked with before had retired, so I informed them we weren't with a realtor yet. "Would you like us to connect you with one?" they asked. I hadn't discussed this with Vicky yet, as they called in the middle of working and she couldn't get away to talk. I said, "Yes," deciding to see where this would lead. I knew we weren't obligated to have to work with whomever they connected me with, and felt it was a safe bet. A moment later, Zillow connected me with Amy, a Preferred Realtor with Zillow. The representative had previously explained that they have a pool to pick from and basically Amy's name was up next. Looking back, I can tell you with one hundred percent assuredness it was God who made the connection. Amy was fantastic. She spoke with me over the phone and arranged to meet us that weekend to view a few of the houses.

Now, Amy wasn't just any realtor. First and foremost, Amy is a strong Christian who attends an amazing church in the area. She has also worked flipping houses on the construction and remodeling side of things. She has been on television — yes, you read that right, she has been on television. She is an amazing family woman with super cool husband and kids. She was way more than just some random

184

realtor Zillow picked for us. Instead, she was the perfect person to help us navigate buying a home, hand-picked by God to help us. God just happened to use Zillow to make the connection, and Vicky and I couldn't have been happier.

$\sim$

The Provision Test...

We had been pre-approved through a mortgage company in California which helped us set the price point for our housing search. On Saturday we first met Amy face to face, looked at three or four houses together but none of them were a definite fit for us. One of them didn't even have a living room, which I'm still surprised at. Throughout the time we spent with Amy, we got to talking about the buying process and the subject of our financing came up. Amy informed us we could stay with the company we already had, but it would make it very difficult to buy a home. The reason was twofold.

First, realtors preferred to work with local mortgage companies in Texas, due to knowing their track record, reputation and ability to work with a realtor and title company on closing the deal. Second, the time difference had been the cause of quite a few deals being unaccepted, due to late responses. She told us we could stay with that company, but simply wanted to let us know what the potential downfalls and risks might be.

This was when the housing market was going absolutely bonkers. Houses were selling within days, well above asking and usually with a bit of a bidding war involved. The main reason was there was an influx of people selling in other, more expensive states, flocking to Texas to buy more room for less money. They could sell their smaller home for half a million dollars, then move here and get a home that was twice the size for half the price, so adding an additional fifty thousand or more to seal the deal was a no-brainer.

It was great for them, but bad for us. Why? Because we had a price cap we couldn't go over, which meant we had to pray hard when we found a home, preparing to move quickly. This meant you not only had to put an offer on the home you wanted, you had to tell a convincing story and be presented as a "sweet" offer for the current homeowners to even consider you.

Sweetening an offer could be a lease back option or paying all the closing costs or having an extremely short (like, *one day*) option period or many other things. Having an out-of-state mortgage company translated to a potentially significant delay, and could quite possibly make it impossible to sweeten an offer and be appealing to sellers. Seeing the look on our faces, Amy recommended a lender she has worked with many times in the past. Unfortunately, I didn't feel the immediate sense of relief I wanted to feel at the time.

Monday morning I reached out to a local mortgage company Amy had recommended. I gave them all the information I had provided to the California company that had approved us before.

This company denied us.

They informed me if I paid off something around $15,000 of our outstanding debt, then we could resume talks with them again. I was deflated and frustrated, and I went to the Lord in prayer.

I didn't get an answer.

Discouraged, I reached out to my pastor so he could join us in prayer. He told me two very important things. First, he believed God *was* going to get us a home. Second, he had just recently bought a new home and had a lender he was pretty sure would work with us. He sent me the contact information and I immediately reached out to Trisha, and within twenty four hours we were pre-qualified once again.

We began looking at homes that met our criteria. Amy's assistant, Isabella, was very instrumental in helping us look. She would send us listings she thought we might like, as well as any listing she got word was newly arriving. In addition, she toured almost every house with us, trying to help us find the home God wanted for us. Fortunately (and somewhat unfortunately), we knew what it felt like to walk into the house and recognize it as the home God had picked for us. This meant we knew what we were looking for spiritually when we toured a house. This also meant we knew what we *weren't* looking for.

There were several houses during the course of this time that we loved in the photos, but didn't get that spiritual connection when we toured it in person. One of our very common sayings (that Isabella probably got tired of hearing) was "We wanted to like this house!"

If you've ever been house hunting, you understand. You're not looking for a house that's the picture-perfect home you would find on greeting cards or in a movie. Instead, you're looking for the *imperfect* perfect home for you. It could be a rustic colonial or a modern design or a ranch or a two story or one in the country or one within a small community or one with three bathrooms or whatever else.

The home is imperfect, but it has character and a variety of areas you will eventually change and repair. It's imperfect, yes, but it's the perfect home for *you*. When God picks the home and you're praying, the moment when you walk into the perfect home is magical. Vicky and I knew anything less than what God wanted for us simply wouldn't work.

On February 12th, we thought we found our home. I thought we had the feeling, as both Vicky and I could see ourselves living in it. It was a great home and well within our budget, giving us negotiating room should we get the chance. The only negative thing was the backyard being flush up against a set of very active railroad tracks. This didn't bother us, however, because the home itself was exceptionally soundproof, enough that you couldn't even hear the train when it passed by as one did while we were there. Oh, you felt the rumble, but that was it. (Looking back, the train coming would have totally spooked our dogs).

We made an offer a little over asking price, hoping the tracks would deter a lot of potential buyers, but in the end the sellers went with another family. So we shook the dust off of our feet, continuing to pray and looking for imperfection.

On March 3rd, we found a house that really felt like it was The One. Both Vicky and I had super strong feelings walking in it. One reason we had such a connection is the home was almost identical to the one my grandmother had bought us previously, except the layout was flipped left to right. Even after just seeing the pictures, I was willing to put in an offer on it. In retrospect, this should have been a red flag for me, because I *knew* I needed to first walk through the house and sense what the Holy Spirit was saying. Instead, I interpreted those house photos as God saying, "Pat, this is the house!"

Isabella suggested writing the current homeowners a letter, expressing our love and interest in their house. Apparently this was something new buyers did in an attempt to establish more of a connection with sellers. After everything was signed and sent, we waited and prayed.

The offers were due the following Monday at noon. I fully believed in my heart this was our house, and we would soon be hearing they accepted our offer. However, this feeling was solely on familiarity and comfort, and *not* on hearing God. In the moment, I'd convinced myself they were one and the same.

They weren't.

The sellers didn't accept our offer.

Honestly, at this point I hadn't realized I was attributing my feelings as hearing from God, and was convinced the sellers were rebelling against what God was telling them to do. In the moment I felt like the devil had stolen something from me. I was frustrated, and went back to God in prayer. He didn't respond with any further direction, but I was reminded of something Pastor Tim Ross has said.

If God tells me to go east and I get to the east coast (of the United States bordering the Atlantic Ocean) and do not receive any additional instructions, then I'm going to get on a boat or a place and continue heading east!
- Pastor Tim Ross (paraphrased)

Without receiving any additional instructions, I continue to "go east," which meant continuing to search for the house God had for us. I did start to feel bad for our realtor team, spending a lot of valuable, unpaid time with us. We never felt anything but love from them, but we felt bad, nonetheless. Vicky and I started going to open houses on Saturdays to hopefully find The One, without wasting more of their time.

On March 23rd, I received a text from Amy, who was equally frustrated with the current market. She expressed she'd had several clients over the last week who'd been outbid. It was a hugely discouraging market for someone trying to get a home — even worse for the realtors. Not only did they have less homes to list, but they constantly wrestled with coming up with a winning bid combination. Before the market insanity, one would put in a bid, and if another bid was placed later, the realtors would talk and an opportunity was given to the lower bidder to raise their bid. Sometimes a "bidding war" would occur, but throughout the process, people were engaged and aware of where they stood, and what they potentially needed to buy the home in question.

No more. Instead, most homes would be listed between Wednesday and Friday, with offers due either Sunday night or Monday morning. Sellers would then sift through *dozens* of offers to decide which one they wanted to take. The individual realtors had no idea if they were coming in as the highest bid or missing the mark by a few thousand dollars (or a few hundred thousand).

Yes, you read that correctly.

Some homes were selling for *$100,000 over the initial asking price.*

Amy sent a text, suggesting we needed to regroup and try to come up with a winning strategy. (Did we already say Amy is the best? 'Cause she is!)

Immediately upon reading her text, God welled up in my spirit. I didn't have a single second to think about a new play or a winning strategy. Instead, I knew God was moving and immediately went to typing out the following reply.

I hear you. But many times it's darkest before the dawn. I hear what you're saying, but like this video says, "It's Friday … BUT SUNDAY'S COMING!" I don't know how or when, but God is providing for us a house. Just this past Sunday a prophet declared that property is coming. So while it's Friday, Sunday's coming. I know that I know that my God is big enough and strong enough and powerful enough that no matter what Friday looks like, Sunday will still come. Miracles will still come. And our home will still come.

I understand what it looks like. I understand what it feels like. I even understand how everything in you and your experience and knowledge can point to "There is no way." But it's Friday. My God is a way maker. And Sunday's coming. Our job is to keep faithful and keep doing what we know we are supposed to do until Sunday gets here. That's how we see the miraculous.

And I personally believe when Sunday gets here, we are going to see a mighty move of God. And until it does get here, let's hold fast to the author and finisher of our faith that he is faithful and able and will have it come to pass. And be listening and watching and praying. In fact, one of the last things Jesus says to the apostles before he is arrested was "watch and pray." Being doing what Jesus told them. I will keep doing what Jesus told me.

The words flowed out of my fingers faster than I could read them or even fully know what they said. In addition, I sent a link to a YouTube video of the "It's Friday... But Sunday's Comin" message (see <u>It's Friday... But Sunday's Comin</u> for text), as that was running all through my head as I was typing. (Ironically, I had to go back and read the text myself so I knew what I was saying.) I knew God was speaking through me in that moment, so I just stepped aside and let Him do it. As it turns out, Amy has heard this message and loved it. While I can't speak for Amy, I believe this really lifted her spirits as well. So we were back to going east and looking for the house.

≈

The Idolatry Test...

In the process of trying to determine what "going east" actually meant for finding a home, Amy and Isabella suggested looking into new construction. The reason was simple: new builds didn't have competing offers to deal with. Instead, you get on a waiting list and when the time comes, you get to purchase a home. In addition, it would have all the latest energy-efficient appliances, windows, insulation, and more. This would bring our energy bills down, as well as our insurance rates.

It all sounded logical, so we made an appointment to talk to a builder on April 12th. However, what I found made me feel... dirty. Because it was a seller's market, the buyer had no say in what was or wasn't in the house. The builders would section off the land and determine which floor plans would be placed on and where. Then they selected all the premium packages to add to the house. Granted, these were some really great things, but you could typically reduce the cost by going with a different countertop style or molding on the ceiling.

Instead, the builders controlled *all* of those details, so a buyer's only option was which of the open lots matched your desired floor plan. This felt wrong to me, like they were taking advantage and gouging us, but this wasn't the worst part. We were later informed that until the house was completed, we weren't locked into a price. This meant the entire time we were on the waiting list (estimating about six months) and the time from initial contract to a move-in, ready home (estimating six to twelve months depending on availability of supplies) they could change the price.

To compound this terrible set up even more, we were informed that the builders were currently raising their prices *between $5k and $20k a month*. The floor plan we'd been looking at listed at about $350,000. If we signed up on a waiting list (say 6 months) and estimating a quick turnaround for building (say 6 months), we could potentially be looking at a final purchase price of $410,000 on the low side, and up to $590,000 on the high side.

When I heard this, I grew sick in my spirit, to the point I felt like I was going to lose my lunch. I knew that I knew that I knew that this wasn't the path God had for us. Fortunately, Vicky felt the same way. We walked out and informed Isabella this wasn't going to be the path for us.

There is absolutely nothing wrong with a shiny, brand new, efficient house. They are awesome. In the best shape possible. You don't have to be concerned something will break within six months or a year of moving in. All the appliances are the latest and greatest, energy-efficient models. There are a lot of really good and cool things about a new build. No question.

However, that wasn't the path God was setting aside for us. We almost ended up prioritizing it before God's plan (like an idol), instead of trusting in Him and continuing to go east and keep searching.

～

The Pride Test...

April 20th. At the advice of our realtor team, we began looking at houses which had been on the market for over seven days. The idea was if new/fresh listing wave passed them over without getting a contract, we might find a hidden gem. This was a fantastic plan, as previously we were looking for whatever immediately hit the market, just like every other potential homebuyer. Vicky was the first to see a home that had white painted brick and blue trim she affectionately called the "My Big Fat Greek Wedding" house. We loved the movie, and the color shouted Greek, plus the colors could always be repainted later if we desired.

Isabella reached out to the listing agent and contacted us later. She was super excited. She said she felt this could be The One, and set up to have us view the house on Friday, April 22nd. One of the potential reasons it was being overlooked was the grass had been replaced with turf. This didn't bother us, and like the paint, we knew we could replace it later if need be.

When both Vicky and I walked into the house, God leapt in our spirits and we knew that we knew that this was the house, from the moment we walked through the door. To begin with, the house was bathed in light. I do not like darkness. I'm not scared of the dark, and I'm fine in dark places, but I grew up in a home where thick, dark drapes covered all the windows, making it feel more like a dungeon than a home. Because of this, I wanted a home to feel light and bright, open and full of life.

This house *exuded* life. As we walked around, we noted how everything on our needs list was being met, and quite a few of the things on our want list as well. For example, there was a pool in the backyard. On top of all of this, the house was listed at $375,000, which was well within our budget. I'd been praying the night before and heard from God the figure $360,000, which would be far too low, practically unheard of in the seller's market. However, I knew what I'd heard, and was going to see what Isabella recommended.

We discovered the house had been sitting on the market for twenty-two days and *no one but us had toured it*. After speaking with the listing agent, Isabella told us she felt we should offer $360,000 —the exact number I'd heard in prayer! We were in, and submitted our offer to the current owners that night.

You might be wondering if pride came into play. There were two ways pride could have potentially sunk us. First, the house was significantly outside of the area we had been living in for over twenty years. Inside the Dallas-Fort Worth metroplex there are communities, areas and even regions. We had been always on the north side, west of the airport, and knew that area really, really well. This house was on the south side, in a completely new place for us.

Living there would feel like moving across the state. Sure, it'd only be thirty minutes by car when not stuck in rush hour, but to us it seemed like another world away. If we had pridefully held on to where we thought God wanted us, instead of being humble to His plan, we wouldn't have found this home.

The second potentially prideful issue was the turf. It didn't bother us, because we knew we could always replace it if we desire. It could have been viewed as a deterrent to making the home move-in ready. However, we humbled ourselves to let God be God, and we couldn't be happier. While this may not seem like a big deal, it was huge to us. This meant being humble and looking at houses outside of our preferred area.

The offer in, we could do nothing but wait.

Previously waiting felt like we were on an elaborate contraption, similar to the ones Batman and Robin would find themselves in, waiting for the candle to burn through the rope that held back the giant axe from slicing you in half. Your mind starts racing, wondering if there was anything else you could have or should have done. Something additional you could have prayed, something you forgot to mention to the realtor. Something you could have done or said when reaching out to the seller. Finally, the timer runs out and you're either elated for escaping the trap or laying there, exhausted and defeated.

Millions of thoughts raced through our minds as the candle slowly burned down and time was ticking by. It wasn't fun. However, I imagine this might also have something to do with the fact that I'm not a very patient man.

This time, however, felt different.

There was no contraption.

No candle. No axe.

For the first time since we started looking at properties, I had zero doubt this was our home. Ironically, Vicky had stated to me beforehand this was the last house she was looking at. If we didn't get this one, she was done. We would just continue to happily live in the apartment. I told her I felt this was different. Sometimes it's hard to convey something you just know to someone, even someone who's super close but just not on the same page.

But I knew. I felt it in my spirit when I'd walked into the house. I felt the confirmation when the realtor suggested the same price I'd heard from God. Finally, I felt it when I put in the offer. All that was remained was to wait for the yes.

On Saturday April 23rd, we were driving down to Austin to visit James at St. Edwards University. As was our custom on the way down, we stopped at the Buc-ees in Temple, TX. For those who may not know, Buc-ees is a gas station, convenience store, food court, clothing store, department store, grocery store and so much more — all in one place. It's not unusual for a Buc-ees to have one hundred pumps and a building that's almost the size of a Walmart in square footage. It also has the cleanest bathrooms I've ever had the pleasure of experiencing.

Because of this, we *always* stop at a Buc-ees and gas up, go to the restroom and grab some snacks. While I was visiting the bathroom throne, of all places, God spoke to me in no uncertain terms. "In faith believing, delete all your Zillow searches."

On the Zillow website/app, you can save searches with your specifications of the kind of house you're looking for. I had a few saved and would periodically get emails and text messages about new homes that fit these criteria. I'll admit that I hesitated at His words for a brief moment, doubt trying to enter my mind. Instead, I pushed it away, and a few minutes later deleted the searches. Why wouldn't I? After all, I knew that I knew that *this* was our house, and I wouldn't be needing those searches. Even if I was somehow wrong and missed God, Vicky had already said she was done, so I still wouldn't need them anyway.

As I exited the bathroom and looked for my wife, God spoke again to me. "By faith believing, buy something for your new house!"

I found Vicky and immediately told her all that God said to me. Both of us were off and looking around the store. Buc-ees had a lot of wall decorations to choose from, of course, and they were all good. However, after looking for about fifteen minutes, we both loved a specific sign. It read, "It's so good to be home!" We bought it along with some drinks and were soon back on the road.

We had a great time visiting with James, albeit way too short. We love our family, and although we get a lot of time with them, it never seems like enough.

Around 5:56pm, when we were about an hour and a half away from returning home, Isabella sent us an audio message. The sellers had accepted our bid!! I immediately texted back, "It's Sunday!" Granted, it was actually Saturday, but as I'd texted Isabella and Amy several weeks prior, Sunday was on the way. God had set this house aside for us, and we were beyond thrilled.

On Thursday April 28th, the inspection was completed. Since the market was still crazy, a typical house contract would have a very, *very* short option period — around one to three days. God graced us with a seven day option period. If memory serves, it actually started out as five and was later expanded to seven. Honestly, I wouldn't have thought much of it, except the inspector was in shock at how quickly it came about. He then went on to share his report: a few big items and a ton of minor little things.

Of the big things, the air conditioning unit was in bad shape. It was the original unit, installed nearly twenty-five years ago, and had seen better days. Then there was some work needed on the pool equipment and a small issue with the electrical system. We negotiated through the realtors to have some of them repaired and the rest left to the sellers purchasing a home warranty. Once that was ironed out, all that was left on our side was to prepare for closing and moving in.

On Friday, May 20th, just a few days before the official closing date of Monday, May 23rd, we received the "Clear to Close" email from our mortgage company. This was such an unexpected and surprising moment, filled with immense joy. Lurking in the back on my mind there was the fear that we would get all the way to the title company and everything would skid to a halt because of something wrong. Of course, I kept rebuking this, because I *knew* this was our house. So when that email came, it was like fireworks had gone off in the clear night sky, just for us.

On Sunday, May 22nd, the day before the close, we had a final walkthrough of the house. This is designed to inspect the repairs and make sure they were done as agreed. We found a few things weren't completed yet. The reason was that we provided a lease back where we closed but the sellers had an extra period to pack up and move out. The people selling felt that they had this additional time to execute all the repairs and did not understand that they were required to be completed before closing. Our realtor informed us that the reason this is required for closing is because once we signed, the sellers were no longer legally bound to complete any remaining repairs and could stiff us with them.

I looked at my realtor and said, "Even if they didn't do anything we agreed on, we're still buying this house!" I said it because I knew this was the house God was giving us, and if we had to do some repairs ourselves? He would work it out.

To be completely honest, the weight around everything was difficult to bear at times, especially the yo-yo pace of submitting contracts and hoping upon hope to finally get a house... only to have it be declined. So when we found many things were still left hanging, combined with the realtor's words, we found ourselves struggling. It was a lot to take, but we kept holding on to the fact God made it clear He had parted the waters for us to get this house. Nothing was going to stop what God had put in motion.

We went out to dinner to celebrate, working hard to keep our focus on Jesus. When I was praying that night, God spoke what I thought at the time was a strange word. "Sometimes God has you fight giants and sometimes He has you stand by, praising Him while God knocks down the walls!" It was strange for two reasons.

First, it was odd God spoke about Himself in the third person. Second, I wasn't sure if God was telling me to go to war about the repairs, or to stand by and watch. He never made that clear, only giving me the statement. Today I believe He was telling me to stand by and watch, but that night, I had no clue what He meant.

Early in the morning on Monday, May 23rd, we received a text from our realtor. She confirmed some of the details about the close later that day, and a few things she'd spoken to their realtor about. All was good and we were good to go.

We arrived at the title company at 9:45am to sign the closing documentation. Our mortgage company does something called "table funding." This means within an hour of the signing completion, the money is at the title company and ready for distribution — a vast improvement when compared to how long it would take in the past.

Before we were taken back with our title officer, we had a brief chance to meet the current owners, and I could tell in those few short minutes that they were super nice people. It also was really super sweet of them to congratulate us on the house and wish us the best. Soon we were taken back to sign all of the paperwork, and an hour later we became elated, ecstatic homeowners.

This is a huge cornerstone in my altar, because it reminds me that it doesn't matter what the storm around you could be, if God gave you a promise, He *will* fulfill it.

I want to be honest, God moved *mightily* throughout this whole process. However, there were many times we were frustrated and discouraged. Many times we would stop looking for new homes, only to return a few days later because we knew we'd heard God.

Today I want to encourage you. If you find yourself in a situation where you clearly heard from God but have not seen the harvest yet… or storms are obscuring the path to the promise… or if the enemy has attacked so much that you want to throw in the towel… hang in there! Your Sunday is coming!! I know it is. God is way too good and full of love to leave you hanging. Just keep moving on.

I like this quote from Dr Martin Luther King Jr, "If you can't fly then run. If you can't run, then walk. If you can't walk, then crawl. But whatever you do, *you have to keep moving forward!*" No matter what, keep moving forward in God. He will always be there with you.

APPENDIX

It's Friday... But Sunday's Comin
It's Friday.
Jesus is praying,
Peter's a sleeping,
Judas is betraying,
But Sunday's comin'.

It's Friday.
Pilate's struggling,
The council is conspiring,
The crowd is vilifying,
They don't even know
That Sunday's comin'.

It's Friday.
The disciples are running,
Like sheep without a shepherd.
Mary's crying,
Peter is denying,

But they don't know
That Sunday's a comin'.

It's Friday.
The Romans beat my Jesus,
They robe him in scarlet,
They crown him with thorns.
But they don't know
That Sunday's comin'.

It's Friday.
See Jesus walking to Calvary,
His blood dripping,
His body stumbling,
And his spirit's burdened.
But you see, it's only Friday,
Sunday's comin'.

It's Friday.
The world's winning,
People are sinning,
And evil's grinning.

It's Friday.
The soldiers nail my Savior's hands
To the cross,
They nail my Savior's feet
To the cross,
And then they raise him up
Next to criminals.

It's Friday.
But let me tell you something:
Sunday's comin'.

It's Friday.
The disciples are questioning,
What has happened to their King?
And the Pharisees are celebrating,
That their scheming
Has been achieved.
But they don't know
It's only Friday.
Sunday's comin'.

It's Friday.
He's hanging on the cross,
Feeling forsaken by his Father,
Left alone and dying.
Can nobody save him?
Ooooh
It's Friday,
But Sunday's comin'.

It's Friday.
The earth trembles,
The sky grows dark,
My King yields his spirit.

It's Friday.
Hope is lost,
Death has won,
Sin has conquered,
and Satan's just a laughin'.

It's Friday.
Jesus is buried.
A soldier stands guard.
And a rock is rolled into place.

APPENDIX

But it's Friday,
It's only Friday.
Sunday is a comin'!

- Easter Meditation by S.M. Lockridge (1913-2000), pastor of Calvary Baptist Church in San Diego from 1953 to 1993.

ABOUT THE AUTHOR

July 12, 1992, an extremely cocky and overly arrogant twenty-two-year-old man entered a small church in upstate New York, utterly unaware his entire life was about to change. Taking his seat, he crossed his arms and sighed skeptically. As the preacher began, a mysterious heaviness entered the room, pressing harder and harder on the man's soul. In less than an hour, he was both broken and restored as he was introduced to Jesus Christ, and from that moment on the man's life has never been the same.

In the thirty plus years that followed, Patrick Aquilone has consistently pledged himself to serve God with all his heart. He's had the privilege of helping plant two churches, leading small and large groups in teaching the Word, overseeing children's ministry, mentoring younger Christians, and pouring his life into many fledgling marriages to help resuscitate them. His heart is to see lives transformed through the amazing power of God.

He earned a bachelor's degree in electrical engineering from Rutgers University and works by day as a software developer. While being born in New Jersey and having met Jesus in New York, Patrick calls the great state of Texas his home, loving both the weather and the people.

Patrick has been married to his wife of thirty-three years and has raised three amazing young adults. In his spare time, Patrick is a perpetual space nerd and scifi geek. He devours all media related to the space race and especially science fiction. His favorite pastime is sitting around a table with friends and family playing board and card game.

facebook.com/patrickaquilone

x.com/patrickaquilone

instagram.com/patrickaquilone